6´

THE IMMIGRANT

by Mark Harelik

Conceived by Mark Harelik and Randal Myler

357 W 20th St., NY NY 10011
212 627-1055

THE IMMIGRANT
© Copyright 1989 by Mark Harelik

Grateful acknowledgment is made to J & J Kammen Music Co., 133 Industrial Ave, Hasbrouck Heights NJ 17604, 201 288-8080, for use of the song *Di Grine Kusine*, Copyright 1922, words by Hyman Prizant, music by Abe Schwartz. Permission must be obtained for use of this music.
All other rights to THE IMMIGRANT are represented by Margaret Henderson, Henderson-Hogan Agency, 247 S Beverly Drive, Beverly Hills CA 90212, 213 274-7815.

THE IMMIGRANT is published in a trade edition by Ballantine Books, a division of Random House, Inc., NY NY.

First printing: September 1989
ISBN: 0-88145-073-1
Design: Marie Donovan
Word processing: WordMarc Composer Plus
Typographic controls: Xerox Ventura Publisher PE
Typeface: Palatino
Printed on acid-free paper and bound in the USA

This play is dedicated to Haskell Harelik,
1887-1987

THE IMMIGRANT had its world premiere in the Denver Center Theatre Company's Source Theatre in February 1985, with the following cast:

HASKELL HARELIK .... Mark Harelik
IMA PERRY .... Ann Guilbert
MILTON PERRY .... Guy Raymond
LEAH HARELIK .... Adrienne Thompson

Director .... Randal Myler
Set designer .... Catherine Poppe
Costume designer .... Anne Thaxter Watson
Lighting designer .... Marty Contente
Stage manager .... Nancy Thomas
Assistant stage manager .... Kent Conrad

CHARACTERS

HASKELL HARELIK *(rhymes with garlic). An immigrant. He arrives at the Port of Galveston, Texas at the age of nineteen. A Russian Jew.*

LEAH HARELIK. *His wife. Three years younger than he.*

MILTON PERRY. *Owner of the Perry National Bank of Hamilton, Texas. A rock-solid, unyielding man. In his late forties.*

IMA PERRY. *His wife. Ten years his junior.*

The scenes, aside from the Prologue, are various locales in and around Hamilton, a tiny agricultural community in central Texas, from 1909 to the present.

NOTE

This play was written in concert with photographs from the Harelik family album. Though there are few references to the use of slide projections, it is intended that a performance of the play be accompanied by the actual images of the actual people upon whose lives this story is based.

PROLOGUE

(The slide projections, and sounds, introduce the countryside of Byelorussia, the heartland of the Russian-Jewish people. We hear a simple balalaika tune, Di Grine Kusine. *The first image we see is that of a young yeshiva boy, six or seven years old. He wears the traditional brimmed cap and tallis. He bears a somber look. Around him, pictures of Jewish village life become images of school, prayer, and the old wooden synagogues.)*

(Intruding into this provincial scene come the sights and sounds of the pogrom—the mad clatter of invading hoofbeats, shouts, and cries. The young boy's image reappears as we see the IMMIGRANT *standing in the center of the stage. The noises whirl around him. We hear whispers of "America; America," and shortly the scenes are those of escape, of train travel, of masses of refugees crowding onto boats in German ports. A lengthy and difficult crossing of the Atlantic, packed into steerage. The arrival at the port of entry. Not Ellis Island, as we might expect, but the Port of Galveston, Texas. The* IMMIGRANT *is lost, hungry, and bewildered. We hear cries of longshoremen, Texan and Mexican, and the general hubbub surrounding the busy port. Banana boats are being unloaded. We hear Texan and Mexican voices hawking bananas.)*

(The blast of a boat whistle blacks out the stage and the IMMIGRANT's *American adventure begins.)*

ACT ONE

Scene One

(Hamilton, Texas, 1909. The clear, tuneful song of a mockingbird brings up the lights on the front porch of MILTON *and* IMA PERRY, *and the street.* IMA *is watering plants on the porch.)*

IMMIGRANT: *(Offstage)* Pananasapennyapiece! Pananasapennyapiece!

(He enters, hauling a ramshackle wheelbarrow filled with bananas, some fresh, some horribly rotten. He is wearing the traditional long, black coat, prayer-shawl vest, and short-brimmed cap of the Orthodox European Jew.)

IMMIGRANT: Pananasapennyapiece!

(IMA stares at him. After a moment, he moves a few feet down the street, then is overcome by sudden dizziness.)

IMA: *(Calling through the screen door)* Milton! Milton! There's somebody out front!

MILTON: *(Offstage)* Who is it?

IMA: I don't know. He don't look good.

MILTON: *(Offstage)* What?

IMA: He looks sick, Milton. You better come look.

MILTON: *(Offstage)* Stay where you are.

(He joins her on the porch.)

MILTON: Hey!

(The IMMIGRANT *has pulled his water bottle from the barrow, its lid dangling. When* MILTON *calls to him, he gestures toward them with the empty container.)*

IMMIGRANT: Kennt ihr mir geb'n ah bissel vasser? *("Can you give me a little water?")*

MILTON: Get in the house. Get.

IMA: Who is he?

MILTON: Do what I say now.

IMMIGRANT: Ich darf ah bisseleh vasser. Nur genook ontsufill'n mein flasch. *("I need a little water. Only enough to fill my bottle.")* Vasser.

MILTON: Oh. Well, you can get some "wasser" at the well at the side of the house. At the side of the house. There. Wasser. Get going.

IMMIGRANT: Pananasapennyapiece!

MILTON: No bananas.

IMMIGRANT: Thank you.

(He goes off toward the well.)

MILTON: Best find some shade!

IMA: Milton, who was that?

MILTON: Banana pedlar. Wandering around, I expect. I give him some water.

IMA: Well, I'll swan....He scared the daylights outa me.

MILTON: No harm long as he keeps moving, I expect.

(He goes inside, leaving IMA *on the porch.)*

IMA: *(With relief)* Well!

Scene Two

(The town square, the next day. The IMMIGRANT *is greasing a frozen axle with a small pot of grease and his fingers. He is quite dirty.* IMA *enters, shopping basket in hand.)*

IMA: Well! Hello!

IMMIGRANT: Hello.

IMA: You were at our house yesterday. My husband gave you some water.

IMMIGRANT: Enschuldig mir. Ich farshtay dir nit. Ich ken nit redd'n Aynglsh. *("Excuse me. I don't understand you. I can't speak English.")* No Aynglsh.

IMA: Oh. Well....Of course. *(Speaks louder)* My husband gave you some water! Yesterday! *(She makes a drinking gesture.)* Water!

IMMIGRANT: Vasser?

(He holds up his water bottle.)

IMA: Yes.

(He offers the bottle.)

IMA: No, thank you!

(He returns to his work.)

IMA: I'd like some bananas, please.

IMMIGRANT: *(Muttering)* Oy. Yetst zeh vill'n koif'n pananas. Zeh vart'n biz meine hent zeinen f'shmutsik mit fetz, un z'vill'n koif'n tsvay toots! *("Now they buy bananas. Wait until my hands are covered with grease and order two dozen!")* Az mi shmirt di reder, geyt der vog'n. *("As you grease the wheel, so rolls the wagon.")* Pananas. Yoh. Pananasapennyapiece. *(He indicates that his hands are too filthy to handle the goods.)* Ich bin tsoo shmutsik.

Shmuts, shmuts, shmutsik! Nehm vos d' darfst. *("I'm too dirty. Dirt, dirt, dirty! Take what you need.")* Uh...take.

IMA: Oh. Well....These look good....

(She takes five and offers him a nickel. He starts to take it and sees how filthy his hands are.)

IMMIGRANT: Ich bin tsoo shmutsik. *("I'm too dirty.")*

(He opens the cigar box and gestures for her to put the coin in.)

IMMIGRANT: Ch'bayte. *("Please")*

IMA: *(Seeing how empty the box is)* Well, I'll swan. *(She drops the nickel in, then points out a nearly blackened bunch.)* Those're getting awful ripe, you know. You really ought to sell those pretty quick. *(She takes them.)* I could make some good bread with these.

IMMIGRANT: *(Taking them from her)* No, no, no.

IMA: Well, they're only gonna get worse on you.

IMMIGRANT: *(With much pantomime)* Diyeh ess ich. Diyeh fa koif ich. Pananasapennyapiece. No pananasapennyapiece. Nit goot. *("These, I eat. These, I sell.")*

IMA: Oh Dora.

(All composure having fled from her charitable impulse, she grabs some hefty bunches and fills her basket ridiculously full. She then hurriedly empties her coin purse into the cigar box.)

IMA: I'm sure that'll cover it.

(She has given him too much money. He grabs a quarter and tries to return it to her.)

IMA: No. No. Nevermind. Much oblige.

(She leaves, flustered.)

IMMIGRANT: *(Calling after her)* Much o-...o-...okay.

(He puts the quarter back in his cash box, then casts a sharp look in IMA's *direction. After a moment's consideration, he exits after her with the wheelbarrow.)*

Scene Three

(The Perry front porch. MILTON *seated with his newspaper. Enter* IMA *with bananas.)*

IMA: Milton...I ran into that pedlar on the square. The one from yesterday?

*(*MILTON *looks at the bananas, then looks at her.)*

IMA: Well, I know. I'll swan if I didn't start buying bananas like I was going into business for myself. I'll make some bread and take it around and you don't get enough fresh fruit besides....

MILTON: *(Returning to his paper)* Still in town, huh?

IMA: Yeah. You know, it don't seem practical to me, hauling them bananas in the sun like that.

MILTON: Well, they look fresh enough to me.

IMA: No, but I mean, Milton, it's not the bananas, it's him. He doesn't even have a horse. He's pulling this wheelbarrow around in this heat with his own back.

MILTON: Yes, well...?

IMA: Well...? I tried to talk to him but he doesn't have any English.

MILTON: No, German, I expect. Now listen, Ima. I know what's on your mind and I'm discouraging you right now. This is not a charitable institution we're running here. Now if the banker's wife adopts every itinerant pedlar that pulls his barrow through town, then what does that say about the banker? Let well enough alone. We run our business and he'll run his.

IMA: No, I know that...

(She peels a banana for him.)

IMA: Here. Have one.

(He takes the fruit and she sees the IMMIGRANT *hesitating at the far edge of the yard.)*

IMMIGRANT: Hello.

IMA: Hello.

MILTON: Get in the house.

(She retreats but doesn't leave.)

IMMIGRANT: Hello. Sir.

MILTON: We've got plenty of bananas. Don't need any more bananas. They're good.

IMMIGRANT: Um...yoh...um....

MILTON: What can I do for you?

IMMIGRANT: No pananas. *(He fumbles around inside his belongings.)* No pananasapennyapiece.

MILTON: *(As* IMA *edges out.)* Ima, did I tell you to get inside?

IMA: Milton, look.

IMMIGRANT: *(He has taken a tightly rolled blanket from his cart. He uses it as a visual aid.)* Ich shloff shoin uff d'ayrd f' die letste tsvay voch'n. Hob g'shloff'n uff d'ayrd. Ich bin farmahtert. Ich hob g'tracht efsher...kennt ihr mir farding'n ah tsimmer? Ich bin nit shtendik cha zoy shmutsik. Shmuts, shmuts, shmutsik! *("I've been sleeping on the ground for the last two weeks. Sleeping on the ground. I'm tired of it. I was thinking...if you could rent me a room? I'm not usually so dirty. Dirt, dirt, dirty!")*

IMA: I think maybe he wants to clean up. Do you want to clean up?

MILTON: No, that's not what he's after. What do you want?

IMMIGRANT: Ich vill ah tsimmer. Ah tsimmer. Ahn orret vie ts'shloff'n. Ts'shloff'n. *("I want a room. A room. A place to sleep. To sleep.")*

(He lies on the ground.)

MILTON: Here now! Get up from there!

IMA: Milton, don't touch him! He might be sick!

MILTON: He's not sick.

(To the IMMIGRANT)

MILTON: I know what you want, and I'm afraid it's not possible. We're not a boarding house.

IMA: Well, Milton, maybe we ought to give him—

(MILTON turns on her.)

IMA: I mean, if he needs something....

MILTON: Ima, I'm proud to help a man who's in trouble. But there's hard times all over and he can clearly fend for himself.

(To IMMIGRANT)

MILTON: No. I'm sorry. No. If you want some water, the well is at the side of the house. Help yourself.

(MILTON turns to go and the IMMIGRANT looks to IMA. MILTON turns back.)

MILTON: Help yourself.

(MILTON heads for the house.)

IMA: Milton....

MILTON: Let's go.

(IMA gives the IMMIGRANT a final look as MILTON herds her into the house. Then:)

IMMIGRANT: Milton!

(They stop.)

IMMIGRANT: Ch'bayte! Vart. Ch'bayte. Milton, gib ah kook. *("Please. Look. Please. Milton, look here.")* *(He pulls a sock from its hiding place.)* Ich vill es nit fahr umzist. Kook. Kook. *("I don't want it for free. Look. Look.") (He withdraws three tightly-rolled bills.)* Gelt! Ich vill dir batsoln ah forroyce. Ich vill dir batsoln. Ich vill zich ohpvasch'n. Ich vill zich rehzieren. Ihr vet mir gleichen. *("Cash. I'll pay you first. I'll pay you. I'll wash. I'll shave. You'll like me.")*

(He offers the money.)

MILTON: Three dollars, huh? It's a poor businessman that offers all his liquid assets for a place to sleep.

(The IMMIGRANT *hides two of the bills behind his back.)*

MILTON: Whoops. The offer's dropping. I'd best sell while I can still get a good price. So one, huh? *(He holds up a finger.)* Only one?

IMMIGRANT: *(Also holds up a finger)* Ayn. Yoh?

*(*MILTON *makes a sound—"I don't know...." The* IMMIGRANT *gestures to the house and makes the same sound.* MILTON *looks at him sharply, but his amusement can be detected.* IMA *laughs, covering her mouth.)*

MILTON: For the night, huh?

IMA: No, Milton! Shame on you.

(She rushes to the IMMIGRANT, *who misinterprets her emphaticness and shies away.)*

IMA: No! Not a whole dollar! I mean....

MILTON: Oh, settle down, Ima. I'm not gonna charge him a dollar for one night.

IMA: Well, you're not even gonna joke about it. You can see he's having a hard time understanding as it is. Now you behave like a Christian.

*(*MILTON *takes a big bite of banana, in response. She addresses the* IMMIGRANT.*)*

IMA: We'd be proud to put you up. Yes. *(She puts her cheek to her hands, indicating sleep.)* Yes.

IMMIGRANT: *(To* IMA*)* Yoh? *(To* MILTON*)* Yoh?

*(*MILTON *shrugs his shoulders and defers to* IMA*. The* IMMIGRANT *is overcome for a moment.)*

IMMIGRANT: Thank you. Thank you! Welcome!! Voo zoll ich avek shtel'n may vaygell? *(He shouts to* IMA *as she shouted to him, earlier.)* Voo zoll ich avek shtel'n diyeh zach!?!

MILTON: Oh! You can put it over by the well. *(Pointing)* The well!

IMMIGRANT: *(Remembering the word)* Well!

MILTON: And while you're over there, wash up. Wasser.

IMMIGRANT: Vasser, yoh!

IMA: I'll fetch soap and a towel. *(She goes into the house.)*

IMMIGRANT: Nu. Ayn, yoh? *(He proffers the dollar bill.)*

MILTON: No.

IMMIGRANT: No?

MILTON: Ten.

IMMIGRANT: Ten?!

MILTON: Cents.

IMMIGRANT: Cents? Okay....Ten cents. *(He fetches his cigar box and counts out ten grimy pennies one by one.)*

MILTON: What's your name?

IMMIGRANT: Ach! Meine papieren! *("My papers!") (He pulls a customs certificate out of his money sock.)* My name. My papers. Chatskell Garehlik. Oif Aynglsh!

MILTON: Well, I'm Milton Perry. And this is my wife, Ima.

(She has returned with a sparkling white towel and a huge cake of white soap.)

MILTON: Now there's just you, isn't there?

HASKELL: Mm?

MILTON: There isn't anyone with you? Brothers or sisters? Wife? *(He points to his wedding ring, then to* IMA.*)* You don't have a wife, do you?

HASKELL: No. No, no.

MILTON: All right, then.

(Behind his back, but visible to the audience, HASKELL *removes his wedding ring and surreptitiously pockets it.)*

IMA: Here you go. Now you scrub up good.

HASKELL: Thank you. Thank you. *(He starts out, then, to* IMA.*)* Shmuts, shmuts, shmutsik!

IMA: Yeah! *(*HASKELL *exits.)* That's good, Milton. Thank you.

MILTON: *(Pours the pennies into her hand)* Here. Put that in the bank.

IMA: Dora.

MILTON: Chaz-kell.

IMA: What?

MILTON: It's his name. Chaz-kell Garlik. He's not German. He's Russian.

IMA: Russian?! Well, I'll swan.

MILTON: Russian. And a Jew.

IMA: *(Silence)* Good heavens, Milton. I wonder if we haven't made a mistake. I mean, I didn't know he was a Jew; I just thought he was down on his luck.

MILTON: Well, your britches just got a little tighter on that one, didn't they? He's paid ten American cents for a bed to sleep in, and a deal's a deal. You just keep your distance.

IMA: Where should we put him?

MILTON: He'll go upstairs.

IMA: That's Charlie's old room!

MILTON: It's an empty room. Might as well get some good out of it.

(IMA *protests.*)

MILTON: Now behave like a Christian.

HASKELL: *(He returns with clean face and hands. He carries the soap and towel, also his cash box and a book.)* Ah! Goot. Goot. *(He returns the soap and towel.)* Thank you.

MILTON: *(Returning* HASKELL's *papers)* Mm hmm. *(*MILTON *goes back to his newspaper.* HASKELL *and* IMA *stand awkwardly.)*

IMA: All right then. The room is right upstairs, Mr. — uh....

MILTON: Garlik.

IMA: Mr. Garlik.

(She goes into the house.)

HASKELL: *(To* MILTON, *showing the certificate)* Garehlik. *(Then, running after* IMA*)* Garehlik. Chatskell.

IMA: Hez-kell.

HASKELL: No, no.... *(He demonstrates the gutteral "ch" sound.)* Ch—Chatskell.

IMA: H—Hazkell.

HASKELL: *('A' for effort)* Yoh, goot! Cha zoy vie ah Yiddishe baleboosta! *("Like a real Jewish lady!")* Ach, Aynglsh.

(He displays the book and reads the title for her.)

HASKELL: "Aynglsh Is Easy". Az ah yohr off im, "Aynglsh Is Easy". *("He should have such a year.")*

IMA: This was my.... *(She gestures around.)* This is for you.

HASKELL: *(Amazed)* Thank you.

(She starts to leave, but he stops her and looks up a page in his primer.)

HASKELL: Good. Night. Ima.

IMA: Good night. *(She thinks for a moment.)* Haskell.

HASKELL: Yoh! Goot!

(She leaves and HASKELL *runs to the door, calling out.)*

HASKELL: Milton! Thank you!

MILTON: *(IMA comes onto the porch, fretting.)* Well, set down and relax, you might as well. You wanted him in, he's in.

IMA: Well. I don't mind him much.

MILTON: *(Sardonically)* Yeah, I expect I couldn't resist him either.

IMA: He's a long ways from home.

MILTON: Long ways. Yes.

(In his room, HASKELL *is practicing from his primer, first reading, then repeating.* MILTON *and* IMA *can hear him out the upstairs window.)*

HASKELL: Good morning. It is a beautiful day. Good morning. It is a beautiful day.

IMA:	HASKELL:
What do you expect he's doing here?	How are you?

HASKELL: How are you?

MILTON: Starting from scratch, sounds like.

HASKELL: I am a stranger here. I am a stranger here.

Scene Four

(The Perry front porch. MILTON *working in the yard.* HASKELL *enters from the well, exhausted. He carries his cigar cash box and one blackened banana.)*

MILTON: Evening, Haskell.

HASKELL: Hello, Milton. (IMA *enters from the house.*)

IMA: Haskell.

HASKELL: Ima. *(He passes her on the porch and shuffles into the house.)*

MILTON: He give me rent money this morning.

IMA: Did he now?

MILTON: Come down to the bank and stood outside 'til somebody called me. Two weeks rent money. For his room, he says.

IMA: Just from them bananas. I'll swan if that boy ain't a natural salesman, then I don't know what. Miz Genther carried me over two dozen of banana muffins this morning. I traded her a loaf of banana bread. If he don't switch to something else, before long this town's gonna swing in the trees.

*(*HASKELL *enters his room.)*

MILTON: I didn't know what to do. He just give it to me.

IMA: That boy's saving hard. He's saving hard and it ain't just for himself, you mark my words. He's got somebody—family or something.

(The focus of the scene shifts to HASKELL's *room. He is writing a letter with a picture before him.)*

HASKELL: Meine fishele Leah, nochamahl shalom f'n d'United States f'n Amerikeh. Un' shalom f'n Hamilton, Texas. Ah toizent tsvay hundert mensch'n...

(As HASKELL *speaks, his recorded voice takes over:)*

HASKELL: *(V.O.)* My sweet Leah, hello again from the United States of America. And hello from Hamilton, Texas—population one thousand and two hundred. Do you remember looking at the maps and wondering what this Texas was? Well, I'll tell you—we had no idea. After the stories we heard of New York, I got off this boat and fell forward into a great open plain. Tiny

little towns. But one of these tiny places appeals to me
very much. Hamilton, it's called. Population one
thousand and two hundred. They have a sign before
you enter the town that tells you this very clearly. How
long would I have to stay, I wonder, before someone is
required to change that number?

The banana business is very good. People here have a
remarkable appetite for this fruit. The produce train
comes to a town nearby, only a two-day walk. And the
bananas I buy — two, three stalks at a time — have
immigrated through the same port at Galveston. We're
both strangers here, these bananas and I, but such
country we've come to. Such wealth. Do you know that
this little town has not one, but two banks? And do you
know something else? I'm living in the house of a
banker. Yes! I've been in my own room, sleeping on a
bed with springs, for a week now. His name is Milton
Perry, his wife, Ima. Strange names, aren't they? Also
strange to be in land with no shul, no rabbi, no Jews at
all. Some days I'm as lonely as a stone. But at other
times, most times, I simply feel free. I sprawl on the
ground and look at the stars as they look at you. Tiny
mirrors that, I used to think, reflect the splendor of
unreachable lands. Now they reflect tomorrow's sun.
The daylight that will fall on the shoulders of your
Haskell. At last, Leah, something is happening.
Something is happening! God bless you and keep you,
my darling Leah, until I can stand by your side again.

(Then live:)

HASKELL: Die tsiet vet avek flee'ehn, meine fishele!
("The time will fly, little fish!")

(The focus shifts back to MILTON *and* IMA.)*

IMA: What in the world?

HASKELL: *(V.O.)* It won't be long.

MILTON: That was him.

HASKELL: *(V.O.)* Haskell.

IMA: Well Dora! You think he's having a nightmare? I don't know, Milton. He's killing himself the way he's scraping those pennies together.

MILTON: Well, it's in the blood don't you imagine? A Jew is tight with a dollar, they say.

IMA: Do they now? Shame on you, Milton. *(She goes into the house.)* Haskell? Haskell?

(HASKELL is placing dollar bills into the letter envelope. He hears IMA calling him and quickly tries to hide the evidence of his correspondence. She arrives at his door.)

IMA: Haskell?

HASKELL: Yes? Hello? *(As she enters, he flips open his primer, grabs Leah's picture, and hides it behind his back.)*

IMA: Hello. I just...uh....You're all right, now? You look awful tired.

(He gestures to the open primer. She's not satisfied.)

IMA: Well....All right, then....Goodnight, now.

HASKELL: Good night. *(She starts to go.)* Thank you.

IMA: Oh. Well, you're welcome.

HASKELL: Much... oblige.

IMA: Well. Yes, indeed.

(She exits.)

Scene Five

(MR. PERRY's office in the Perry National Bank building. MILTON is seated at his desk, smoking.)

HASKELL: Mr. Perry?

MILTON: Yes? Oh. Come in, Haskell. Have a seat. Take off your coat.

(HASKELL *does so reluctantly.*)

MILTON: Uh, you wanna...?

(He indicates HASKELL'*s cap.)*

HASKELL: No! No, no.

MILTON: Okay....Well, how do you like our little town?

HASKELL: Oh, good. Very good. I like...this place.

MILTON: Not quite the same as it is in Russia, is it?

HASKELL: No. Hot. And safe.

MILTON: Safe? Well, now I never thought of that. No, there's not much trouble around here.

HASKELL: No.

MILTON: Sit down, Haskell. I'll be right with you. *(He completes some work.)* All right now, Haskell. I'm sorry to pull you away from your, uh, banana cart and all, but I felt it was necessary that we talk a little bit. Now Haskell, you've been our guest, so to speak, for nigh onto a month now —

HASKELL: Six...

MILTON: What?

HASKELL: Six weeks. At Tuesday. Six weeks.

MILTON: Is that a fact. So. I have to say that I haven't been aware of much progress on your part.

HASKELL: I....

MILTON: Now just let me tell you what I'm talking about. I can see that you work hard with this...this banana business of yours and my wife has opened her house to you and I'm not saying you're not welcome. But your stay in our home was never meant to be a permanent situation and I hope that's not your impression.

(Pause)

MILTON: Now, you want a home of your own, don't you? A home? A house? Where you live? A house? You want your own —

HASKELL: *(Gesturing to the surrounding office)* A house. Yes. It's fine.

MILTON: Good.

HASKELL: *(Indicating* MILTON's *desk)* It's good!

MILTON: Fine! Well, the point is I watch you bust your butt hauling that load of rotten bananas around —

HASKELL: Bust...bust....

MILTON: Bust your butt....

HASKELL: Butt.

MILTON: Yeah, your butt. Your ass. This thing.

(Gestures vaguely. HASKELL *comes over to look.)*

HASKELL: Yes?

MILTON: No, no! Haskell, would you just sit down.

HASKELL: I don't know.

MILTON: I know you don't. Just sit.

*(*HASKELL *does and realizes "butt".)*

MILTON: Look, Haskell. I feel that the way you're conducting your business...business?

HASKELL: Business, yes.

MILTON: ...is impractical.

HASKELL: Im...?

MILTON: Not. Not practical.

HASKELL: Not...?

MILTON: It's not efficient! Your bananas go bad too soon. That thing weighs a ton. You're busting your — breaking your back. You have to sell at too high a volume to turn a profit. Not good. Now I want to ask you something, Haskell. Do you intend to stay here? Stay in Hamilton?

HASKELL: Stay? Yes, I stay....

MILTON: Are you prepared to take some advice? Because I can't approve of the way you're going about this.

HASKELL: Tell me.

MILTON: All right then, look. Get rid of those bananas. It's my feeling that a lot of your trade in the county has come from people just trying to help you out. And that won't support a business. It's bound to give out. But what people do need is what we call notions and sundries.

(HASKELL *doesn't understand.*)

MILTON: Pots, pans, brooms and things!

HASKELL: Yoh!

MILTON: There isn't a housewife in the county that doesn't need something like that every —

HASKELL: Mr. Perry. Listen. This kind business I know.

MILTON: Good! Now there's a fellow in Waco —

HASKELL: In Russia, mens do this. Sell for house. To the lady. Sometime cart. Sometime —

(He searches for the word.)

HASKELL: — not cart. Carry. This mens we see him. This town. This town. This town. No house. No place. We call him luftmensch. Mens of air. Dirty. Lost. In Russia, he is sad mens. I say — never. Never like this. I come to America. To this Texas. And I do same. The cart. The walk. Carry. But no pots. No little string. No medicine. Fruit!

MILTON: Now, wait a minute, Haskell.

HASKELL: In Russia, nothing like this bananas! Yes cart. Yes walk. Yes dirty. But fruit! Sweet....

MILTON: Haskell, you're not listening —

HASKELL: Mr. Perry! More fruit! Put more fruit!

MILTON: More fruit?!

HASKELL: Yoh!

MILTON: Goddamnit Haskell, I'm trying to talk you out of the fruit —

HASKELL: No, no! Different!

MILTON: Different?

HASKELL: Different kind! Many different kind!

MILTON: Now wait a minute.

HASKELL: Put the...the, uh....

MILTON: Wait just a blue-eyed minute! Sit down, Haskell. You know you may be right? Why not turn that barrow into a goddamn fruit store. You could cut back the bananas —

HASKELL: But the bananas...!

MILTON: I didn't say chuck 'em, I just said cut back. And then work in apples and oranges and peaches, maybe. And grapefruit! You ever hear of grapefruit?

HASKELL: Grape? Sure, for wine.

MILTON: No, no, no. I mean grapefruit. Big! Big yellow things. Grow on trees.

HASKELL: Big yellow things....

MILTON: In the valley, they have orchards and orchards—all right, Haskell, you want fruit? Then goddamn make it fruit!

HASKELL: Yes, it's good!

MILTON: Good? Son, it's great. It's perfect. Now, you're still gonna have a heavy load, but a horse'll take care of that. Less spoilage and your diversity'll turn a greater profit. Now that's the American way.

HASKELL: Yoh. Not just America. Good....

MILTON: Good sense.

HASKELL: Sense.

MILTON: Well, that's just what I'm talking about. Now there's a shipper in Galveston we can contract with. And your conveyance will need some modification.

HASKELL: What does it mean, this mod-...mod-....

MILTON: Changes! Changes, Haskell! Some rows of shelves, and....(*He grabs paper and pencil.*) Look — a wagon. All right?

HASKELL: Yoh?

MILTON: Shelves. Two sets. On both sides. And room in the front and back for baskets and what-not. And a little roof on it, like this. And on top, a sign, maybe.

HASKELL: Yoh! Put the, uh...the, uh....

MILTON: Your name.

HASKELL: Garehlik!

MILTON: "Garlik's Fruit and Veg...." "Garlik's Fruit." No, that'll never work. Harlik. "Harlik's Fruits and Vegetables." How's that sound?

HASKELL: Eeh....

MILTON: And a horse. A horse to pull it.

HASKELL: That's good! You draw very good!

MILTON: Haskell, you're right. If you're going to be a businessman, then by God, be a businessman and not a manual laborer. Now does that interest you?

HASKELL: Yes!

MILTON: Good sense?

HASKELL: Yes.

MILTON: Damn right! You're smart, Haskell. You work hard. I don't want to see you break yourself down.

HASKELL: Yes. It's a good idea.

MILTON: You bet it is.

HASKELL: But no.

MILTON: No?

HASKELL: Idea is free. Two shelf, one horse not free.
Cost money I don't —

MILTON: I know that. I'm going to loan you the money.
The horse and wagon'll be mortgaged to the bank and
you'll pay me back. A little bit at a time. Now what do
you think?

HASKELL: What do I think. I think yes.

MILTON: Now listen. You shoot straight with me and
I'll help you. You don't and you're out on your butt. Do
you understand that?

HASKELL: Butt, yes.

MILTON: Good. Good boy. Now I'll draw up a proper
contract, we'll sign it in the morning and get started.

HASKELL: Good business, Mr. Perry. I give back.

MILTON: Not another word, Haskell. We're..."partners"
now.

(*He offers his hand.* HASKELL, *amazed, takes it.*)

HASKELL: Partners.

(HASKELL *picks up the drawing.*)

MILTON: And a partnership is built on trust. You don't
jew me and I don't jew...

HASKELL: (*Immersed in the drawing*) It's good!

MILTON: Sorry.

HASKELL: Sorry?

MILTON: Nothing. I'll see you at home.

HASKELL: At home, yes. You draw very good!

(HASKELL *exits.*)

Scene Six

(The Perry front porch. IMA *is waiting as* MILTON *enters the yard.)*

IMA: Would you hurry up, mister? We're gonna be late for church.

MILTON: Ima, you know I'm not going.

IMA: Now, why not, Milton? I thought you said you were coming with me.

MILTON: Why would I say anything like that?

IMA: I wish you'd come.

MILTON: Ima, I didn't go with you last week. I'm not going with you next week. It'd be plumb silly for me to go with you this week.

IMA: You go ahead and make light, mister. You're gonna be awful sorry when your day comes.

MILTON: *(As he disappears into the house.)* I'm sorry already.

*(*IMA *exits. As the following letter begins,* HASKELL *brings his new cart into the yard. A sign above the cart says "Harelik's Fruit and Vegetables". The produce is arranged along shelves and in baskets. It is the end of the day and* HASKELL *throws a tarp over the cart before going inside for the night.)*

HASKELL: *(V.O.)* My precious Leah, I love to write to you. I hate to write to you. These months see only paper and ink passing between us and between times I pretend that I am with you, talking. I hear you reply. I answer. "It's dark now, Haskell. Time to come home, yes?" "Yes, you're right. I'm on my way." "And shouldn't you dress more warmly?" "You're sitting in Russia. Don't tell me how to dress in Texas." "My,

Haskell! You're so stern!" And then my sternness falls to pieces and we kiss. But the kiss falls on paper and ink. I hate these letters.

(HASKELL *goes into the house.*)

Since I last wrote to you, we've moved into the new establishment. We've added several rows of shelves. Oh yes, and we've added vegetables now and a new roof. And to the staff, we've added one horse. Very docile. No back-talk.

(HASKELL *enters his room, dons his skullcap and prayershawl, and begins his evening prayers.*)

I assume you've opened the other envelope. Yes, it's true. Sit down. Stop crying. Part of the money will buy train passage from Minsk to Bremen. If they give you trouble at the border, you have to sneak across, I'm afraid. Be prepared for that. The ticket is for steerage passage from Bremen to Galveston. You'll like steerage. Very pleasant. If you're lucky, they won't lock you in. If you're luckier still, you'll get a top bunk. Be strong, Leah. Forget politeness. Forget respect. Forget sleep. And for God's sake, don't carry more than you can hold at one time. Travel light, Leah. Travel as light as you can. Once in Galveston, the Texas Flyer Train will take you to Gatesville, where I'll be waiting.

Oh, hurry, Leahle *(Lay-eh-luh)*, hurry. It's getting harder and harder for me to concentrate on these letters. Or on anything else these days. During my prayers, even, I drift away and daydream.

(*A mockingbird sings outside his window. It distracts him, but he returns to his prayers.*)

Listen! Do you hear?

(*It sings again.* HASKELL *tries not to listen.*)

A bird with the most beautiful song in the world met me at my boat, led my every step to Hamilton, and currently resides outside my window. A mockingbird, it's called, and it sings with such piercing sweetness that I think my heart will break.

(It sings again. HASKELL *breaks off his prayers and stands at the window.)*

HASKELL: *(V.O.)* That bird calls to me as I call to you. "Leave the past. Leave it. Travel light. Kiss your Mama goodbye and don't look back."

(He removes his prayer shawl.)

I've awakened into my dreams, my love, and I can hear you beyond the horizon starting your long walk toward me.

(He removes his skullcap and stands at the window.)

God bless you and keep you and take a deep breath! The next time you hear from me will be in person! Haskell.

Scene Seven

(Before dawn. HASKELL *enters from the house. He removes the tarp from his produce wagon, then proceeds to remove the sign atop it. It is punctured by a large, jagged hole. He still wears his short-brimmed cap, but the prayer-shawl vest is conspicuously gone.)*

IMA: *(O.S.) (From within the house)* Haskell, are you still here?

HASKELL: Yes, I'm just... still loading up.

(He hastily puts the sign on the ground and throws the tarp across it as IMA *appears in the doorway.)*

IMA: Oh, good. Haskell, I need six more of them green apples. I'm gonna make another pie. I've got dough left over and we might as well keep one for ourselves.

HASKELL: Yes, ma'am. Six green apples.

(She leaves the pie she has been holding on the porch and comes into the yard. She holds out her apron, making a basket.)

HASKELL: That's five cents.

IMA: Five? Are you sure?

HASKELL: First customer of the day gets special price.

IMA: Now I don't want you giving away another of your —

HASKELL: No, no. It's good business.

IMA: 'Cause you need to save every nickel.

HASKELL: I save nickels. Pennies, too.

IMA: You must be sending to your folks.

HASKELL: Mm hmm.

IMA: In your letters.

HASKELL: Yes.

IMA: Good. Well, all right then, here you go.

(She pays.)

Oh, Haskell, I have an apple pie that needs delivering and I'd be much obliged if you could carry it for me.

HASKELL: Yes. That's fine.

IMA: Oh, good. *(She goes onto the porch to get it.)* I'm sending this out to poor old Miz Haggerty. She busted her hip chasing a hen across their pasture. Slipped in a wet cowflop and practically snapped in two.

(He takes the pie.)

IMA: I'd have to laugh if it hadn't hurt her so bad. Now, she's out in Lime Rock, you know.

HASKELL: Miz Perry, I can't take this pie.

IMA: Oh Haskell, we could find room somewhere, I'm sure.

HASKELL: Please. I can't take it. I'm not going out to Lime Rock today.

IMA: Well, I don't understand. You've been going out there every day. *(She sees the damaged sign on the ground.)* What in the world...?

HASKELL: My customers on that road, they change their mind.

IMA: Is this a gunshot? Haskell, what in the world happened to you? Isn't this a gunshot?

HASKELL: Yes.

IMA: Good Lord in heaven, boy, did somebody take a shot at you?

HASKELL: No! Not at me. It was just, just to scare me, or....

IMA: The Peterson boys.

HASKELL: I don't know! I was on the road to Lime Rock. It's a long stretch, you know. It was green and cool, and the birds and the horse sound like Russia. And I daydream.

(A distant, ghost-like balalaika is heard.)

HASKELL: I thought I was there. And then I hear other horses and the hoofbeats are very fast and I get scared because this too is a memory I have. And then all of a sudden here are five, six men and they stop me and shake the cart and say...things. People I trade with. I know them, but...something, they...show me their guns and shoot this hole in the sign and I run like hell. So. They scare me, I run. Maybe it's just fun, but I don't think I go back to Lime Rock today.

IMA: Haskell, you tell me who those men were and we're going to do something about it right now. I just can't believe that Christians would behave like that.

HASKELL: No, no.

IMA: Yes! We'll put a stop to it.

HASKELL: No, I just don't go back there.

IMA: Nonsense, Haskell. It's the Peterson boys, I'm sure of it.

HASKELL: Miz Perry, please! Forget this. If we make trouble, it will get worse. I promise you, I know this. Please. It would anger them and you....

IMA: Well, I'm ashamed, Haskell. We're just not used to...strangers. Some don't handle it like Christians. It frightens the daylights outa me, Haskell.

HASKELL: Yeah, scares me, too. I'm not a brave man. Even a tiny thing, I cut my finger, it bleeds, it makes me sick. I get scared, I run. I don't go back. It's not the first time.

IMA: You amaze me, son. You leave your home, travel thousands of miles, put on a new language, eat my cooking. If that's not courage.

HASKELL: It's not courage. It's just running. And your cooking is very good.

IMA: Well, you better say so. All right, you better hitch up and run along. You're losing daylight. *(Something catches her eye.)* What're you selling here, hornet's nests?

HASKELL: Hornet? Oh! No, no hornet nest. This is a brand-new vegetable.

IMA: Well, I'll swan. I didn't know there could be such a thing.

HASKELL: Oh yes! Brand new. Hard-to-choke.

IMA: Say again?

HASKELL: *(Holding up an artichoke)* It's called hard-to-choke.

IMA: And you eat 'em.

HASKELL: Yes!

IMA: How?

HASKELL: I don't know. But it's new! I was too curious, so I buy them and everyone says, "My Lord! What is this?" And I say, "Hard-to-choke", and no one can believe it.

IMA: Well, I don't believe it. Easy-to-choke, more likely.

HASKELL: Here. You take it. *(He places it in her apron.)* If you can figure how to cook it, no charge.

IMA: Well, I'll give it a try. You're back early tonight.

HASKELL: Oh yes, Shabbos.

IMA: And that means Sabbath, don't it?

HASKELL: Yes! Very good! Shabbos, Sabbath.

IMA: Shabbos. It's such a pretty word. They sound so much alike, there's hardly any difference between the two.

HASKELL: *(With a glance toward Lime Rock)* Almost. So if the horse is still on his feet and I don't work him too hard, maybe we get home in time.

(He exits.)

IMA: Yes, all right. *(Looking after him; worried, wondering)* Goodbye, then.

Scene Eight

(The new shop on the square, a regular storefront building, housing Harelik's Fruits and Vegetables. MILTON is carrying, dragging actually, large bags of flour, rice, and potatoes into some semblance of order. He is beat and irritable. IMA enters from the street.)

IMA: Well, they told me you were over here hauling beans. I had to come see for myself. My.

(The place looks pretty bleak.)

IMA: The place looks nice....Get these shelves filled up some, it'd be right proud. Is this all there is?

MILTON: There's another load coming over this afternoon.

IMA: Oh, good. Where's Haskell?

MILTON: Driving the load.

IMA: Oh, good. Milton, I wish you'd be careful. This suit's gonna be a mess.

(She tries to dust him off.)

MILTON: Ima.

IMA: Well, why're you doing all this by yourself, anyhow? I thought Haskell took on a boy to help him out.

MILTON: He took on a boy, Ima. He's in the back doing the same thing I'm trying to do. Do you expect a ten-year-old child to do it all by himself?

(He stalks into the back room.)

IMA: *(To herself)* Bite my head off, why don't you?

(A crash is heard.)

MILTON: *(O.S.)* Goddamnit!

IMA: Please don't cuss. It's good of you to help out, anyway.

MILTON: *(Re-entering.)* Yeah. Helping out like a mule helps a plow.

IMA: A good work is its own reward, Milton.

MILTON: *(He glares at her.)* Don't you preach at me, woman. I'm here, aren't I? Playing papa all over again? It's just not exactly what I had in mind. Now are you prepared to accept that?

(He rests.)

IMA: Well, it looks real nice. I'm glad to see him get permanent. Now at least he don't have to go looking for trouble. If folks want to trade, they can come to him.

MILTON: That's the question, isn't it?

IMA: Mm. *(She gazes out the window.)* You know, I've never seen this town so close 'til he come. Kinda sets off the difference, I guess. I was afraid of him, was you? First time I heard him bucking out them evening prayers of his, I thought he'd raise the devil, for sure.

MILTON: Well, didn't he?

IMA: How do you mean?

MILTON: Them Peterson boys and the like?

IMA: Oh, come now, Milton. Those boys are purely mean.

MILTON: Yes, but he sure brought it out of them easy enough.

IMA: Milton!

MILTON: Well, goddamnit, there's a truth to that! I'm standing in front of the whole town to set up a Jew in business — I don't know if anybody'll put one foot in this place. The families in this county have been here a long time. And we're not used to a foreigner — Mexican, Niggra, any kind.

IMA: It's un-Christian, Milton.

MILTON: Yes. So's he.

IMA: Shame on you. That's not what I meant.

MILTON: Well, people change hard, is all I'm saying. And this stuff rots.

(HASKELL *has entered during this last exchange. He is wearing work clothes and a straw work hat. When he doffs it after entering, he is bare-headed. He will remain bareheaded for the rest of the play.)*

IMA: Haskell! Scare me to death.

MILTON: Well, let's get the load in.

HASKELL: No, stay. Stay just a minute. I need to consult with you. And you too, Ima. Please. *(Gesturing to them both)* Sit. I think the business is growing very well. Who would think? We start from a stinking little wheelbarrow and now, thanks to both of you, here is this store full of goods, with a mortgage — a real American business. Soon, God willing, I move to my own house, but unfortunately not yet, so much money has to go here and —

MILTON: Haskell, I told you not to worry about that and I meant it.

HASKELL: Yes, well, thank you. So....

MILTON: So?

HASKELL: ...so, I feel that with one employee — a good one — a good boy, yes?

MILTON: Yes.

HASKELL: — that with one employee, the work is easier, is more efficient and, and, and practical....

MILTON: Haskell, for Chrissake, what is it?

HASKELL: So we need another employee.

MILTON: I'm getting back to the bank.

HASKELL: Milton, I think it's a good idea.

MILTON: Haskell, it's a very bad idea. It would be stupid to put on more help. You've been open for one day and —

HASKELL: I've been open for eleven months! I work hard....

MILTON: This is ridiculous. I'm not gonna hear any more of this.

(He starts for the door.)

HASKELL: Milton, please! My new employee—

MILTON: Your new employ... I don't believe this.

HASKELL: —is my wife.

(They are stunned.)

HASKELL: From Russia.

IMA: I knew it.

MILTON: You've been deceiving us, boy.

HASKELL: No, no. Every day I was going to tell you....

IMA: That's where your letters have been going.

HASKELL: Yes.

MILTON: And the money.

HASKELL: Every week.

MILTON: So you're bringing over a wife.

HASKELL: Yes.

MILTON: And you thought it'd just be a nice little surprise for us.

HASKELL: Mr. Perry, I want to tell you many times, but you keep giving me help and I owe you more and more money.

MILTON: You're goddamn right you do.

IMA: Milton, be careful.

MILTON: No, you be careful. I trusted you, son.

HASKELL: You can still trust.

MILTON: How many more of you are there?

HASKELL: Only my wife!

MILTON: Now, am I supposed to believe that?

(Pause)

IMA: You should have told us, Haskell.

HASKELL: I tell you now.

MILTON: When it's too late.

IMA: Milton.

MILTON: Well, our hands are tied. When does she get here?

HASKELL: She's outside. In the wagon.

IMA: Well, bring her in, Haskell. She's burning up out there.

HASKELL: *(He goes to the door and turns back.)* You can rely on me, Mr. Perry. The risk is the same.

MILTON: Yeah.

(HASKELL goes. As the PERRY's wait, we hear:)

HASKELL: *(Offstage)* "Zeh vill'n dir bahkennen. Ich vill dos trog'n. Gib mir. Dos iss unser neier krom. Vos klayost deh? Koom arein, fishele. Koom arein. ("They want to meet you. I'll carry that. Give it here. This is our new shop. What do you think? Come in, fishele. Come in.")*

(HASKELL precedes her, carrying a wicker case and a large clanking bundle. LEAH enters, clutching two candlesticks. She is small and frightened.)

HASKELL: My wife, Leah. Hob nit moireh, fishele. Zog eppes. Zog zeh gut morg'n. ("Don't be afraid, fishele. Say something. Tell them good morning.")*

MILTON: Hello.

IMA: Hello.

(Immobile, LEAH looks slowly at the PERRYS, at the store, at HASKELL. She opens her mouth but no sound emerges. She begins to panic. Her distress grows until the only things she sees are her candlesticks. The people and the room disappear and she is left alone.)

Scene Nine

*(A balalaika is heard as scenes of the Hamilton town square
are projected. The few objects in the grocery store are eerily
lit. LEAH's travel clothing melts away and she is left in her
nightgown. It is several months later. Her candlesticks gleam
as if with an inner light. She picks one up and seems not to
recognize it.)*

LEAH: Ach, mei' Gott, siz ah meshugenneh velt. *("Oh,
my God, it's an insane world.")*

HASKELL: *(O.S.)* Leah?

LEAH: Ah meshuggeneh velt.

HASKELL: *(Entering)* Leah, what are you doing?

LEAH: *(Examining a candlestick)* Vos iz dos? *("What is
this?")*

HASKELL: What?

LEAH: Vos ruf ihr dos f'n Aynglsh? Diese leichter?
("What do I call this in English? These candlesticks?")

HASKELL: It's a candlestick.

LEAH: Ah candle shtick. Ah candle shtick? Ich verde
meshuggeh. *("I'm going crazy.")*

HASKELL: Leah...

LEAH: Ich bin ahnahr, Haskell. *("I'm stupid.")*

HASKELL: Leah, what's wrong? You're not stupid.

LEAH: Nit in mei' sprach, ober listen at me f'n Aynglsh.
F'n Yiddish, I can speak, I can think, I know what to say
it. But f'n Aynglsh, ich veiss nit vos dos iz. Ah candle
shtick. Mei' Gott. *("Not in my language, but listen to me in
English. In Yiddish, I can speak, I can think, I know what to
say. But in English, I don't know what this is. A candle stick.
My God.")*

HASKELL: Fishele, it takes time. It's hard. Speak Aynglsh. It will get easier.

LEAH: Haskell, where are we?

HASKELL: Where are we? We're at home. In our own place.

LEAH: But where are we? Us.

HASKELL: *(He tries to usher her from the room.)* Leah, come back to bed. It's cold down here.

LEAH: Ich bin nit ah kint, Haskell. *("I'm not a child, Haskell.")*

HASKELL: I know you're not a child, Leah.

LEAH: Something terrible's going to happen.

HASKELL: Leah, has someone treated you badly? Said something to you? Called you names?

LEAH: No, Haskell, no.

HASKELL: Well, I don't understand what—

LEAH: Look, Haskell! Look at this town! There must be thousands of places where we live.

HASKELL: Where we live?

LEAH: Where there are Jews.

HASKELL: Oh, Leah, please. We've talked about this....

LEAH: No. Nobody says things, but I'm in the street so different. People they come in, they talk to me. They make me stupid. Are you so perfect? Don't this bother you, too?

HASKELL: Yes, of course, Leah, but what can we do?

LEAH: Lohmir avek geh'n, Haskell. *("Let's leave, Haskell.")* Let's find our own people.

HASKELL: But Leah, the store, our business...

LEAH: Business. Another word to learn.

HASKELL: Leah, what the hell is happening?

LEAH: Look at you. Is your head covered? When did this stop? We don't eat kosher—

HASKELL: Now damnit, Leah!

LEAH: —we don't eat kosher, you don't pray at sundown—

HASKELL: What difference does that make, Leah?

LEAH: What difference? You're a Jew. I married a Jew.

HASKELL: So I'm still a Jew. Did I change in the night? Did I grow a tail? I know it's hard here, Leah,—

LEAH: It's impossible.

HASKELL: It's not impossible. So we don't keep kosher. My head is uncovered. I don't want to be strange, either. These people are our customers. They buy, we eat. Do you think God will hate me for that? Why does he need me to wear a little piece of cloth on my head? In twenty years, I'll wear a toupee, He'll be happy.

LEAH: Mei' Gott, you make a joke about it. It's nothing to you.

HASKELL: So what do you want, Leah? We should go back to Russia?

LEAH: We were happy.

HASKELL: We were not happy! You were a child in your mother's arms. You saw nothing.

LEAH: Even a child sees, Haskell. I knew what was happening.

HASKELL: So what do you suggest we do?

LEAH: You should take care of us, Haskell. Is everything only for you?

HASKELL: Where, then?

LEAH: I don't know. New York.

HASKELL: And where do we run from there? And from the next place, where do we run?

LEAH: Then there is no place for us?

HASKELL: Leah, here is our place! I'm not going to run again! No more running! Even a coward has to stop and say our place is here! That's the end! Yes?

LEAH: *(Pause)* I'm alone. Mei' Gott, I'm alone. *(She stares at him for a long moment, then picks up a candlestick.)* I would polish these up, they could shine in the dark.

HASKELL: They're beautiful.

LEAH: Why? Two pieces of junk. Sell them, see what you can get. *(She flings the candlestick at him.)*

HASKELL: Leah!

LEAH: What is left? Speak Aynglsh? Make a joke? If being a Jew means owning two candle shtick, then I don't want it! I don't want it! I don't want the baby! I don't want you!

HASKELL: *(Silence)* Leah. A baby.

LEAH: A baby, Haskell. We'll turn him loose like an animal.

(She panics and tries to run from the room. HASKELL *physically restrains her. She screams.)*

HASKELL: No. No, no, no. Leah. A baby.

LEAH: What do we do?

HASKELL: What do we do? Thank God. We rejoice! *(He embraces her.)* I don't see anything. When does it happen?

LEAH: Where will we go?

HASKELL: Leah. Mama. Do you know what I found out? Do you know that Hamilton is only a little over fifty years old? Where did these people come from? You think Americans are only Americans. They, too, came from someplace else. Germany, Italy, everywhere. They were alone. Moses led the Israelites into a strange land.

LEAH: So now you're Moses?

HASKELL: I'm not Moses. I'm just saying, we're not the only ones.

LEAH: Haskell. I don't care about the past, who came from where. For my baby there is no life here. Yes, of course, I can learn to live in a different house. I learn a different language. I can say Howdy, grow cactus in a front yard. But my baby, Haskell, will not make these shortcuts. To cover his head, do I buy a cowboy hat? Pointy boots, big belt buckle? He'll fit right in, huh?

HASKELL: Our baby won't be without God, Leah! This child will be a Jew. I don't know how. But when this person, this little Jewish person is born, we will have brought something new, something old into a different corner of the world. How many years have the Jews been wandering? Who says we can't wander to Texas and rest for a while?

LEAH: Yes, Moses.

HASKELL: *(Sings)* Tsu mir iz gekummen ah kusine
Shayn vie golt iz zie gevain, di grine
Beckelach vie roite pomerantsen
Fiselach vos betten zich tsum tantsen —

LEAH: It's like I never got off the boat.

HASKELL: *(Sings)* Zie iz nit gegang'n nor geshprung'n
Zie hot nit gerett nor gezung'n —

LEAH: I'm still looking for land.

HASKELL: *(Sings)* Fraylich lustik iz gevain ihr meene
Ot azoy gevain iz mein kusine —

END OF ACT ONE

ACT TWO

Scene One

(In the blackout, we hear the Calvary Baptist Church congregation singing a vigorous version of "Where Shall I Be?" *Lights reveal* IMA *in her kitchen. She is singing with the music and, as it fades away, continues the hymn alone. She is preparing a vegetable stew.* LEAH *appears, quite clearly nine months pregnant.)*

IMA: Oh! Leah! You scared me! What is it? Are you feeling all right?

LEAH: I was...tired, I guess.

IMA: Uh, are you...?

LEAH: I'm not really tired...I was...I wanted to go home, but Haskell sent me over here.

IMA: Well....Why don't you....You want to lie down? You can use your old room.

LEAH: He told me to come help you.

IMA: Oh. Well...I've got a world of vegetables to get into this pot.

LEAH: I'm not much good.

IMA: What, honey?

LEAH: I'm stupid. I just....

IMA: Here you go. *(She gives* LEAH *an apron.)* Dora. Would you just look at these carrots. One thing I'm sorry is Haskell let go of his grocery business.

Somehow he always had the best things. Stuff you'd never seen before, sometimes.

LEAH: His back is no good. The bags are too heavy. At home, never....

IMA: Well, he'll do right well with the new dry goods. He's a good businessman. We like him.

LEAH: I know.

IMA: *(Handing her a knife)* Here. I'll skin and you cut.

(LEAH indicates for IMA to place the knife on the table. LEAH then kisses her right thumb and tucks it firmly into the apron's waistband. She takes the knife and tries topping a carrot, but she's clumsy left-handed. She puts down the knife, kisses her left thumb, tucks it in the waistband, and tries cutting right-handed, but this time the carrot wants to roll away. IMA grabs the carrot to steady it. LEAH cuts the end off and IMA turns it around. LEAH cuts the other end. IMA drops the topped carrot into the enamel pot she's holding. There is a resounding plonk. They start on another interminable carrot, when a mockingbird calls from out the window.)

IMA: Hello! *(As IMA leans toward the window to call to the bird, she knocks over the salt shaker. Without thought, both women grab a pinch and toss it over their shoulders in an identical fashion. They regard each other.)*

IMA: Just for luck, you know.

LEAH: Yes. We do that, too.

IMA: Well...luck is luck. Don't matter where, I guess. You got to laugh at that, though. Now why do you suppose it's going to do any good to throw more salt around after you've already spilled it? Seems like it'd be luckier to clean it up.

LEAH: Maybe that's why they do it.

IMA: That's why...what?

LEAH: To clean it up.

(LEAH brushes all the spilled salt into her hand and flings it all over her shoulder.)

IMA: Well, you're most prob'ly right. Anyhow, we got good luck coming to us now.

LEAH: Kenahoreh! *(She spits once — and hard.)*

IMA: *(Looking carefully at her floor)* What was that?

LEAH: Oh. Nothing. It's....

IMA: Oh. Well...all right.

LEAH: Kenahoreh.

IMA: Uh huh. Is that...?

LEAH: Yiddish. Jewish. Kenahoreh. You say that to...when you don't want the...the evil eye.

IMA: Honey, I hear you talking, but I'm stumped.

LEAH: You said we got good luck coming to us and I said kenahoreh because it means no evil eye because it's bad luck to wish for good luck. You'll attract the evil eye.

IMA: Canorry.

LEAH: Kenahoreh, that's right.

IMA: Listen, I got one of them words, too.

LEAH: You do?

IMA: Padadooly.

LEAH: What does it mean?

IMA: I have no earthly idea. My mama was a very superstitious woman. I'd hear it a dozen times a day.

LEAH: Padadooly.

IMA: I don't know what's supposed to happen when you say it. Nothing, I 'spect, if it's working. Well, in fact, you want to see something superstitious, you looky here.

(IMA lifts the hem of her skirt to reveal her hidden talisman.)

LEAH: What is it?

IMA: Well, it's a rabbit foot.

LEAH: Really?

IMA: Well, yes. I've worn this'n or one like it every day
of my life since I was at home.

Do not depend on a rabbit foot
Nor get your hopes up too soon
Unless it is the left hind one
And was caught by the light of the moon

'Course I don't know if this'n's regulation or not. Silly.
But you never know.

LEAH: Yes. That's why I do this. *(She kisses and tucks her
thumb as before.)*

IMA: So you don't get the...canary.

LEAH: Kenahoreh — that's right.

IMA: Well, Dora! If I didn't wonder.

LEAH: I've never....This is my first....

IMA: Honey, you just go right ahead.

LEAH: No, I mean...I was scared. And...I'm not so scared
now.

IMA: Scared of what? *(She reads* LEAH's *face.)* Dora! Not
me! Well, I got to laugh at that. There's not enough of
me to be scared of. *(*IMA *makes an accurate guess.)* I'm a
Christian?

(A distant, ghostlike balalaika is heard.)

LEAH: When I was little, in Bobruysk, most of my
friends were Gentile. We lived near a Catholic church
and we play there and run around and who knew the
difference? Once a priest walked by in his black cassock
and black hat and his beard and he didn't look no
different from the rabbi, to me. And my friends, they
ran up to him and kissed his ring. So what do I do? I
don't want to be left out. So I ran up to him and kneeled

down and kissed his ring and he patted my head and
my mother gave me the worst beating of my life.
Someone would put up a sign. "Brothers in Christ! If
you love Holy Mother Russia, you will get rid of the
Jews!" I love Mother Russia, too.

(Silence. The mockingbird sings. LEAH *looks for it.)*

LEAH: What is that one?

IMA: That's our mockingbird.

LEAH: Even the birds are different.

IMA: I come a good piece myself. Not so far as you, but
pretty far.

LEAH: You're not from Hamilton?

IMA: Canton, Missouri. A little bitty river town on the
Mississippi and made to get out of, let me tell you. My
papa was the first to go. He ran off barefooted after
Mama buried his shoes and wouldn't tell him where.

LEAH: She buried his shoes?

IMA: Well, if your husband's sorta light-foot, as they
say, you take and bury his shoes somewhere near the
house and he'll stay home. Least 'til he finds 'em. She
did the same thing with our dogs.

LEAH: She buried their shoes?

IMA: She cut off the tips of their tails. Buried 'em under
the back porch. Now that seemed to work. She never let
me sleep with my doll. Said it'd dance on my head in
the night and make me crazy. Dora. I tell you who was
the crazy one. Hamilton, Texas, still wasn't far enough
away from her.

LEAH: It's far away for me.

IMA: Well.

LEAH: I loved my Mama.

IMA: It was a backwards life.

LEAH: I'd hang on to her. Really. Hang onto her dress while she was cooking or...and she would send me outside, but I'd sneak around to the window so I could just watch her.

IMA: Well, that's silly. You should get out and play.

LEAH: Do you have children, Ima?

IMA: No. Yes. Of course. Now why did I say that? I had two boys. I lost one early on and the other, Charlie, is...left home. Left his crazy ol' mama behind. Like I left mine. Well now, if I didn't forget the onions. There's just no flavor at all without the onions.

(Pause. LEAH *watches* IMA.*)*

LEAH: You know, I can't believe she cut the tails off those —

IMA: Those dogs? Oh, Dora. Our neighbor? Her husband got the TB, so she tried to make up a tonic for him where you had to boil down a live dog.

LEAH: The dogs had a pretty hard time there!

IMA: No, you didn't want to be a dog in Canton. Now some of those old superstitions there was some sense to. Like I remember she'd never let us eat fish and milk together. Now that'll make you sick.

LEAH: We have that!

IMA: You do?

LEAH: Well, sort of that. We don't eat milk and meat together. I mean, we used not to.

IMA: Did it make you sick?

LEAH: No. It's not kosher.

IMA: What's that?

LEAH: Kosher? It's certain foods you can't eat.

IMA: Well, you see? It's the same thing.

LEAH: No, it's not the same at all! It's in our Torah. It's
the Jewish law. I mean, yours was superstition, but we
believe that. But I don't understand Haskell. He's so
quick to say "We've got to change. We've got to change.
It's not possible here." If it's something you believe, you
can't just throw it away. It's part of you. And once that
is gone, then what am I? And what will my...?

(She tries to withhold her tears.)

IMA: These're pretty strong onions, aren't they?

LEAH: Yeah.

IMA: Now, you're gonna laugh at this. Take a piece of
the outside skin. Take one.

(LEAH does.)

IMA: And put it on your head. Do it.

(She does.)

IMA: Now, that'll keep it from burning your eyes. Is it
working?

LEAH: No.

IMA: All right, I got one more. Mama always had a
backup. No, leave that there. And hold this matchstick
between your teeth. Now say padadooly three times.

LEAH: Padadooly. Padadooly. Padadooly.

IMA: Is it working?

(LEAH shakes her head.)

IMA: Well, a lot of those old notions — just hocus
pocus...just plain hot air.

LEAH: If it's nothing but hot air, how come you still
wear that rabbit's leg?

IMA: Well, I wouldn't want to be foolish, child.

(LEAH, finally unable to withhold herself, weeps bitterly.)

IMA: Honey, there's some things you just don't let go of.

(IMA, *also unable to withhold herself, lightly touches* LEAH's *arm and* LEAH *grabs her, burying her head in* IMA's *breast. She cries, then begins humming.*)

IMA: What's that you're singing?

LEAH: When I get upset, Haskell sing it to me to calm me down. It works better when he does it.

IMA: Sing it.

LEAH: It's about a girl who comes to America. Red cheeks and dancing feet and all she learns is to stop dancing. She don't have such a very good time.

IMA: Sing it.

LEAH: *(Very haltingly, she illustrates the words for* IMA.*)*
Tsu mir iz gekummen ah kusine
Shain vie golt iz zie gevain die grine
Beckelach vie roite pomerantsen
Fiselach vos betten zich tsum tansten

(LEAH *stands and begins a little dance.*)

LEAH: Zie iz nit gegangen nor geshprungen

(She takes IMA's *hand and they slowly begin a circle.*)

LEAH: Zie hot nit gerait nor gezungen

(LEAH's *face begins to glow and they circle faster and faster.*)

LEAH: Fraylich, lustik iz gevain ihr meene
Ot azoy...!

(Suddenly LEAH *is contorted by the first of her major contractions.* IMA *rushes to her, throwing her arms around her.*)

IMA: Well, honey, it's about time.

Scene Two

(The Harelik front porch, very late at night. The front door is propped open with a small chair and LEAH's *cries are clearly heard from within.* HASKELL *paces the porch. He calls inside.)*

HASKELL: Ima? Miz Perry?

IMA: *(O.S.)* Yes, Haskell, what is it?

HASKELL: I called Dr. Cleveland over an hour ago. I don't know what's taking him so long.

IMA: *(Appearing at the door)* He's in here, Haskell. You let him in some time ago.

HASKELL: I did?

IMA: Yes.

HASKELL: Oh, good.

*(*IMA *attempts to go back inside.)*

HASKELL: How is Leah?

IMA: She's fine. Listen, Haskell, you want us all to come out on the porch? We could talk a lot easier that way.

*(*MILTON *appears at the edge of the yard.)*

IMA: Milton!

(She goes to him. In a hissing whisper:)

IMA: What took you so long? He's like to turn inside out.

MILTON: All right! I'll set with him.

IMA: I should hope so.

(She goes back to the porch.)

IMA: Whyn't y'all visit for a spell? It might be very relaxing.

(She goes in. Silence.)

MILTON: The place looks good, Haskell.

HASKELL: Mm hmm.

MILTON: You're quite a gardener.

HASKELL: What?

MILTON: You're quite a gardener. The place looks good.

HASKELL: Well, it's not me. Leah plants the garden.

MILTON: Well, I don't mean just...I mean...the bushes and things. That magnolia's really taking hold — Damnation! *(A loose porch step has nearly dumped him on the ground.)* What the hell's wrong here?

HASKELL: Oh, I know. I put a couple bricks there. They slip out.

MILTON: Well, I'd take a little better care of things before somebody breaks their neck!

(A sharp cry is heard from LEAH.*)*

HASKELL: Ima! What was that? It sounded real bad!

IMA: *(O.S.)* Haskell —

HASKELL: Is she all right?

IMA: *(O.S.)* Haskell, would you relax? She's fine!

HASKELL: I'm relaxed!

*(*IMA *appears in the doorway.)*

HASKELL: Does she have to scream?

IMA: Listen, Haskell, would you like to come in and help for a while? Hold her hand or something?

HASKELL: Yes! Of course, I will!

IMA: Just keep the noise down.

HASKELL: Excuse me, Milton. They need me for a minute. Relax.

*(*IMA *and* HASKELL *exit.)*

MILTON: I'll be right here.

(More cries are heard from LEAH. HASKELL *reels out of the doorway,* IMA *following.)*

IMA: Here, bend your head over. Breathe through your nose. Sit. Stay.

(To MILTON*)*

IMA: He'll be more help out here. You keep him quiet!

(She goes in. A mockingbird sings.)

MILTON: You're waking up the whole neighborhood here. You know if you whistle at it, a mockingbird will pick up your tune and sing it back to you? You wanna give it a ...? Here. Listen.

(He whistles. The bird sings something entirely different. He tries a different whistle. The bird sings something different again.)

MILTON: See? Haskell. Thought about a name?

HASKELL: Matleh.

MILTON: Mmm hmm. That a boy or a girl?

HASKELL: Girl.

MILTON: Yeah, I figured it was. It's nice.

HASKELL: Yes. My grandmother, may she rest in peace.

MILTON: Yes, indeed. And if it's a —

HASKELL: Mordechai.

MILTON: Oh, that's a good one. Relative?

HASKELL: No, Bible.

MILTON: Ah.

HASKELL: He was an uncle of Esther.

MILTON: Now which one is she?

HASKELL: Queen Esther! Saved the ancient Jews from Haman!

*(*LEAH *cries out.)*

MILTON: *(Calling across the street)* Hello, Miz Castle!...No, everything's fine....Nope, nothing yet....Yes, Ma'am, soon as we know anything....No, no trouble. We just got a loose step here. *(Muttering)* Yeah, we'll get a man right on it.

(A baby's cry is heard.)

HASKELL: I can't stand it! My God, when will it stop?

MILTON: Haskell.

HASKELL: I can't take this!

MILTON: Have a cigar!

(The baby is heard again.)

HASKELL: Leah!

IMA: *(O.S.)* Haskell! *(As HASKELL runs into the house, he nearly knocks IMA down at the door.)* Oh! *(She sits, exhausted. MILTON, too, sits.)* A boy. They're fine.

MILTON: You made it just in time.

IMA: How'd you manage to keep him in his skin?

MILTON: Did my bird imitation.

HASKELL: *(Banging through with a bundle)* Excuse me, please!

(He places the baby in the middle of the yard.)

IMA: What in the world are you doing?!

HASKELL: Put the baby on the ground!

IMA: What?!

HASKELL: For good luck! Touch the baby to the ground.

IMA: Well, pick it up! It's been there long enough!

HASKELL: Mordechai. Welcome to America.

MILTON: Esther's uncle.

IMA: Esther who?

Scene Three

(The scene is the same, 1917. MILTON *is in the porch chair.*
HASKELL *is at the door, as* LEAH's *cries are heard from
within.* MILTON *watches* HASKELL *fret his way into the
yard.)*

MILTON: Well, I'll tell you one thing. This young Doc
Cleveland is a damn sight more reliable than his daddy.
You know Charlie, our youngest, come all by himself?
I'd run my fool head off to fetch old Doc Cleveland, and
by the time we got back, Charlie was just settin' there
looking at us. And that old fart charged me for the full
delivery just the same.

(He steps on the same bad step and it gives way as before.)

MILTON: Goddamnit, Haskell, haven't you ever fixed
this thing?

HASKELL: Oh. We always use the other side.

MILTON: Jesus Christ, son! And you with a pregnant
wife walking up and down this thing twenty times a
day.

HASKELL: Yes, I'm sorry. I should fix it. The bricks slip
out.

MILTON: *(He gets on his knees, peering under the step.)*
Look. Look here. This whole piece is busted out.

HASKELL: I know it's busted! That's why I put the
bricks —

MILTON: The whole damn place is falling down!

HASKELL: Yes, I'm sorry!

MILTON: Well, hell! *(*IMA *appears at the door.)*

IMA: Would you-all hush your language out here? I'd
shut the door, but she says it'd keep the angels from

helping the baby, so you're just gonna have to pipe down!

HASKELL: How is she?

IMA: She's working hard. She's fine. Now hush up!

(She goes in.)

MILTON: Sometimes that voice irritates the hell outa me. You talk about something to vibrate your skull, Ima's "Cavalry" Baptist. Wednesday nights and twice on Sunday. She got me to go a couple of times, but I tell you, everybody in there's got a voice like that.

HASKELL: Miz Castle came into the store today, said she was praying for us and our poor children.

MILTON: How's that?

HASKELL: I don't know. She's Church of Christ. Maybe they're concerned about these unbaptized children being born.

MILTON: Yeah, well, bunch of do-gooders out stirring up some good to do. Ima's been raggin' my butt to get baptized. Used to, she didn't bring it up so often, but the older we get....

HASKELL: Why is it so —

MILTON: Important? Why you'll go to hell, son. Straight to hell.

HASKELL: Sounds bad.

MILTON: Yeah well, given my choices I'm not so sure.

(A sharp cry from LEAH pulls HASKELL's attention.)

MILTON: Got a name picked out?

HASKELL: Well, if it's a girl, Matleh.

MILTON: Oh, yeah,...

HASKELL: My grandmother.

MILTON: Your grandmother, that's right.

HASKELL: And a boy would be Moishe.

MILTON: Moishe.

HASKELL: It's Yiddish for Moses.

MILTON: Mordechai, Matley, Moishe....You're gonna give Church of Christ the fits.

IMA: *(In the doorway, smiling)* Haskell?

HASKELL: Oh, my God! So soon?

IMA: So soon? Well, we got bored in there and —

(HASKELL rushes past her.)

IMA: — all right, hold on, Haskell, I know where you're headed.

(She heads into the yard and spreads out a small quilt she's been holding. HASKELL dashes out with the baby. She guides him to the quilt.)

IMA: I don't know why y'all insist on this. It can't be good for the child.

HASKELL: Moishe.

MILTON: Another unbaptized Texan.

Scene Four

(The scene is the same, 1922. LEAH's cries are heard. Discovered are HASKELL and MILTON on their hands and knees at the porch steps. A small, brightly embroidered blanket is spread on the lawn. MILTON pounds away with a hammer.)

MILTON: Okay, now, I think that fits. Put some weight on it. Careful.

(HASKELL kneels on the step and MILTON hammers.)

MILTON: All right, now. Got another nail?

(It is hammered into place.)

MILTON: Now, by God, I think she'll do.

(MILTON *backs off and steps on the same place as before. It gives way as before.*)

MILTON: God bless America! All right now, what the hell happened?

IMA: *(Appearing at the door)* All right now, look. I can't shut the door 'cause it'd keep the angels away, so you're gonna have to just stop construction.

MILTON: Well, never mind, Haskell. We can prop it up with these bricks.

IMA: Why're you doing this in the middle of the night, anyways?

MILTON: It needed fixing.

IMA: Dora. *(She exits.* MILTON *stands on the step, testing it. It holds.)*

MILTON: I believe bricks is the answer, Haskell. You're gonna get a much solider base with these bricks under here.

HASKELL: Milton, have you tried one of my jujubees?

(*He runs to the edge of the yard and back, having picked two small fruits.*)

MILTON: One of your what?

HASKELL: Jujubees. I planted this when Morty was born, but it's taken this long to make anything out of it. Here, taste it.

MILTON: Looks like a date.

HASKELL: It's a desert fruit. They grow them in Palestine. We have this tradition to plant trees. Someone is born, you plant a tree. Someone dies, you plant a tree. Someone plants a tree, you plant a tree. Now, the jujubee is for Mordechai. That plum tree is for Moishe. And I'll have something for this one. They say it's to show a faith in the future. Children and trees —

they take a long time to grow into something, so you must have faith in the future.

MILTON: Sure. You hold a baby in your arms and you think everything's gonna turn out blue skies. Our Charlie? Out battin' around from one skunk hole to another? Just turned on me. Run off.

(Pause)

HASKELL: I ran away.

MILTON: Yes, but.

HASKELL: Well, I left my parents. May they rest in peace, I practically left them to die. But I saw everyone growing twisted and for my children, I want something else. What am I if not for my children? Still, you don't know what's inside that seed when you plant it.

MILTON: I never could talk to him. Never knew what was inside him.

(A baby is heard from within. IMA appears on the porch with a bundle.)

IMA: All right, Haskell, you got the blanket spread?

HASKELL: Yes, Ma'am, I do!

IMA: Then come a'runnin'.

(She hands him the bundle.)

IMA: Three boys in a row.

MILTON: Well, damn. Your grandmother's gonna be mighty disappointed.

HASKELL: She's been dead fifty years. She can take it.

(He hands MILTON the bundle.)

HASKELL: Quick, put him on the ground.

MILTON: Wait! Now hold on a minute. Isn't that your job?

HASKELL: Special circumstances.

MILTON: What circumstances?

IMA: Honey, they've named him Milton.

MILTON: That's too bad. You've gone and ruined him for sure.

(He places the baby on the blanket.)

HASKELL: It's another boy, Miz Castle!...No, she's been expecting for the last nine months....Yes, I'm sure of it. Will you come see him tomorrow?... Wonderful....Thank you!

(He turns to look at the PERRYS with his baby boy.)

Thank you.

Scene Five

(At the blackout of the previous scene, we hear "Roly Poly"—the recording by Bob Wills and the Texas Playboys. As the song plays, we see projected photographs of Mordechai, Moishe, and young Milton as young boys, then older boys, then young men. In various shots they are posing, clowning, playing. We also see LEAH and HASKELL grow older. The house grows older. The town grows older. What we see is an American family stretching its wings. Toward the end of the song, LEAH is discovered at the HARELIK dinner table, set for the Sabbath meal. It is 1939. The silver candlesticks gleam. The challah rests beneath its ceremonial cover. LEAH busies herself, checking her watch, looking offstage. She then places a kerchief on her head, lights the two Sabbath candles, and recites the blessing beneath her breath. As the song ends, the final photograph is of Mordechai, Moishe, and young Milton holding their mother high off the ground. She is laughing. LEAH removes the kerchief and calls out.)

LEAH: Haskell, everybody! Supper! (HASKELL, IMA, *and* MILTON *come into the room. To* HASKELL:) Good Shabbos. We couldn't wait.

HASKELL: Oh, sweetie, I'm sorry. *(He kisses her.)* Good Shabbos.

(The same greetings are exchanged with MILTON *and* IMA.)

LEAH: That's means "Have a good Sabbath."

IMA: Like Merry Christmas.

LEAH: That's right.

*(*LEAH *and* IMA *move to the table.* MILTON *speaks confidentially.)*

MILTON: Haskell, did we hold you up here?

HASKELL: No, no, no. Shabbos starts at sundown, so we have to light the candles before it gets dark.

IMA: You still have those beautiful candlesticks, honey.

LEAH: Oh, no! I'm not letting go of these!

HASKELL: *(Indicating her seat)* Ima, please.

MILTON: So the day doesn't start in the morniing?

HASKELL: No, the day starts at night.

LEAH: *(Indicating his seat)* Milton.

HASKELL: I mean, the day...not the day, but the beginning....

(He looks to LEAH.)

LEAH: Our holidays begin at sunset. When the sun sets, it completes the old day.

(There is a white skullcap on HASKELL's *plate. He puts it on.* MILTON *examines the white skullcap on his own plate.)*

HASKELL: It completes the old day, that's right. I mean, the morning is still the morning.

MILTON: Well, that's a relief.

HASKELL: That's a relief, so good Shabbos.

HASKELL: It completes the old day, that's right. I mean, the morning is still the morning.

MILTON: Well, that's a relief.

HASKELL: That's a relief, so good Shabbos.

(MILTON *holds the skullcap curiously.* HASKELL *takes it from him and begins to pocket it.*)

IMA: No, no, Milton. You wear one, too. They've never had us in on shabose before. Might's well do it right.

(MILTON *puts on the skullcap.*)

HASKELL: Ready?

MILTON: Let 'er rip.

HASKELL: All right. The first thing is the blessing for the children.

LEAH: Who aren't here.

HASKELL: We bless them anyway. They need it.

LEAH: They all left to go deer hunting with the Tolberts. I don't know.

MILTON: Oh, Tolbert'll keep a good eye on 'em. They've got a real nice stand down near Lampasas.

LEAH: I like them to go, get outside, but —

HASKELL: Milton pesters us to buy a gun. All their friends have guns. You say no, but —

LEAH: Oh, and cars! If they can tear all over the place in someone's car, heaven! And little Milton is the worst.

(MILTON *rejoices.*)

HASKELL: Milton's not the worst.

| HASKELL:
All right, we're getting
off the track here. | LEAH: *(To* IMA*)*
He goes out,
he stays late. |

HASKELL: All right, the children.

(*He recites the blessing.*)

LEAH: I am, too. It's really perfect. The kids are away. We don't hardly see you no more.

IMA: I know it.

HASKELL: Now, this prayer is called the Kiddush. It's the blessing of the Sabbath.

IMA: Shabose.

LEAH: That's right!

IMA: It's such a pretty word.

MILTON: All right, quiet now. Let the boy do his business.

(HASKELL *recites the Kiddush.*)

LEAH: Now we say omayn here, but it's the same as amen, so....

(*They all say one or the other.*)

HASKELL: Now, this means, "Blessed are You, O Lord God, King of the Universe. You gave us the commandments, You, uh...."

LEAH: "...You gave us the holy Shabbos to remind us of the Creation, to remind us of our liberation from Egypt; we, who are Your chosen people...." Oh.

HASKELL: There were a lot fewer people then, I think. It was an easier choice.

LEAH: "Blessed are You, O Lord God, Who makes the Sabbath holy."

MILTON: All right, now. That's very nice.

HASKELL: And we drink the wine.

(IMA *balks.*)

MILTON: Oh now, Ima. I think this'd be an exception, don't you?

IMA: (*To* HASKELL *and* LEAH) Well now, I'm embarrassed, I guess. Baptist Church doesn't drink. Ever.

LEAH: Oh, honey! I didn't even think of that! Of course, it's all right. Here, give me the glass. Maybe some fruit juice....

IMA: Oh, now I feel bad. I just hate to insult your beautiful little ceremony.

HASKELL: Ima, it's no insult.

IMA: I'll make an exception.

LEAH: No, no.

IMA: I'll make an exception. *(To* MILTON, *with an edge)* This is just between us and the candlesticks. *(She raises the glass.)* All right then, down the hatch or whatever.

MILTON: I don't think down the hatch is quite what's called for.

HASKELL: L'Chayim.

MILTON: L'okay.

LEAH: To life. L'Chayim.

ALL: L'Chayim.

MILTON: And many more.

HASKELL: Yes, sir.

(They drink.)

IMA: Ooh! That's strong! It's good, though. I mean, the aftertaste is very —

*(*MILTON *is smirking.)*

IMA: Oh, hush up!

HASKELL: And the last blessing is for the bread.

(He uncovers the shining challah loaf. He recites the blessing and as he passes pieces to all:)

LEAH: You have to break it off, because if you cut it with a knife, —

IMA: —you get the canary.

LEAH: Right.

HASKELL: Blessed is the Lord God, King of the Universe,...uh....

LEAH: Who brings forth the bread from the earth.

HASKELL: Thank you, professor, Good Shabbos everybody, now let's eat.

LEAH: All right! There's the bowls. Haskell, serve the borscht. There's bread and butter and here are — *(She uncovers the serving dish.)* — the blintzes.

MILTON: Uh huh.

LEAH: Now, don't look for the meat, these are all cheese.

MILTON: So it's just....What is it?

LEAH: Oh! It's blintzes.

(She serves one to MILTON.*)*

LEAH: A blintz.

(She serves one to IMA.*)*

LEAH: Two blintzes.

MILTON: A blintz.

LEAH: It's from the old country.

HASKELL: They're delicious.

LEAH: You see, they're like real thin kind of pancakes wrapped around this sweet cheese.

MILTON: Sweet cheese.

IMA: Well, I don't think we've ever come across —

LEAH: Now here's applesauce, here's sour cream. You can mix a little or just separate, either way.

MILTON: And this is....

HASKELL: Borscht.

LEAH: Spinach borscht.

MILTON: Borscht.

LEAH: It's a cold soup.

IMA: Oh. Well, that fresh dill smells delicious.

LEAH: So, eat.

HASKELL: Now, Milton, I want you to try this blintz with a little applesauce on it.

(He spoons some onto MILTON's *blintz.)*

MILTON: Is that good on there?

HASKELL: It's delicious. Now you just taste it.

MILTON: Applesauce on the blintz. Okay....

*(*MILTON *gives it a try as everyone watches.)*

MILTON: Well, that's good. Leah, that's delicious.

HASKELL: Now, will you relax? They're fine. All day she's been worrying.

LEAH: Well, on Shabbos, we like to eat just dairy, so I didn't know.

IMA: *(Having sampled the borscht)* Well, honey, this is just delicious. I mean it. It's real good.

LEAH: Oh, thank you. It's still strange to have so much meat. Every day, practically.

HASKELL: Because in the old country, we'd get a chicken, sleep with it for a week, we were so happy.

IMA: It must have just been awful.

HASKELL: There's no word to say how it was. Was it awful? You fear for your life. Oh, yes. All the time. And with another monster on the loose in Europe, it's hard to stop thinking about it.

LEAH: Ooh, when I think of that Milton yesterday....I haven't seen you that angry in years.

IMA: What'd he do this time?

LEAH: We were listening to the radio and all of a sudden, the music stops and we hear this announcement and they say that Hitler is dead. That somebody got into his headquarters and killed him.

MILTON: When, you heard this yesterday?

HASKELL: We were crying and laughing and dancing around. We couldn't believe it. And then by accident, I knock over the radio and what do I see? Two little wires. And where do these two little wire lead? Milton's bedroom.

LEAH: They hooked up this microphone to have some fun with us.

HASKELL: Microphone!

LEAH: Hitler is dead. Haskell took his belt after him.

HASKELL: But the frightening thing is he thought it was funny.

MILTON: Well, a boy'll find a joke in just about anything.

HASKELL: Yes, but to him there is no danger. He is safe. Whatever is happening is far away — oceans away, and so he makes a joke. It scares me. Not just my son. Most people, I think.

MILTON: Most people what?

HASKELL: Think they are safe.

MILTON: Where?

HASKELL: Here.

LEAH: Now, Haskell, mach nit a gantz'n tsimmes. *("Don't make a big deal.")*

HASKELL: Who's making a tsimmes?

MILTON: What exactly are we in danger from, Haskell?

HASKELL: There's Hitler, there's Mussolini.

LEAH:	MILTON:
He's very angry about it.	You're talking about a real localized conflict there.

IMA: HASKELL:
Well, he's talking to   How can you say it's
the original America First.   localized? It involves
                                  all of Europe.

MILTON: Then it's a real European conflict. We're a long ways off from there, Haskell.

HASKELL: Not as far as you think, Milton.

MILTON: You stick your nose into other people's business and you're gonna get it whacked off. There's no reason to involve the rest of the planet.

HASKELL: (To IMA) Am I involving the rest of the planet?

IMA: Dora! Don't drag me into this. I don't know nothing about it.

LEAH: It's just a frightening thing, Mr. Perry. They say thousands are being killed.

MILTON: Now wait just a second. Let's not work it around so I have to defend these bastards, excuse me. The only reason I'm on about this is you know Roosevelt is trying to involve us in this thing and I think it would be the biggest mistake.

HASKELL: You think it's a big mistake, it still might be the best thing to do.

MILTON: That's right. Raise taxes and start wars.

HASKELL: Finish wars.

MILTON: Same difference.

IMA: Maybe you two would like to settle this out in the yard?

HASKELL: Milton, you're just like the kids with the radio. There's nothing bad happening here, so why worry? We'll wait 'til they're at the city limits, maybe Mr. Tolbert'll loan us a deer rifle.

MILTON: Oh, Haskell.

HASKELL: Well....

IMA: It's a savage world, I guess. Makes life in Hamilton seem awful quiet.

LEAH: I love it here. I would never leave.

HASKELL:
The reason it's quiet is the world stops at the city limits.

MILTON:
Hamilton is quiet because we've managed to avoid getting into everyone else's business.

HASKELL: Milton, you have to put some of your concern out into the world.

MILTON: Haskell, what the hell are you on about? You're an American now.

IMA: Milton, don't start something.

MILTON: May I talk, please? You don't live there anymore. You're here. Forget about it.

HASKELL: I can't forget.

MILTON: You've been here thirty years.

HASKELL: They're my people.

MILTON: Then why didn't you stay there and fight it out? Why did you have to run off?

IMA: He didn't mean it like that.

MILTON: Don't apologize for me.

HASKELL: Because we were being killed off, Milton. We had no way to fight back.

(Silence)

IMA: We're very lucky to have you here.

HASKELL: And we're lucky to be here. It almost sounds like an accident, doesn't it?

MILTON: An accident.

LEAH: Haskell, it's not an accident. It's God's blessing.

MILTON: Haskell, I seem to remember you had some help along the way.

HASKELL: Milton, I don't forget that. I'm not ungrateful. But after a while, after many years, in fact, of accepting gifts and giving thanks, instead of filling you up, it makes you smaller. You have to be able to give back. This is what fills you up. And the one thing I would most like to give, I can't.

IMA: What is that, Haskell?

HASKELL: Freedom. Share my freedom with my own people. As an American.

MILTON: Where would you put them?

HASKELL: My God, Milton, what is all this land, this space around us? The wealth is embarrassing.

MILTON: Well, how long would that continue to be the case if we brought in a million starving people every year? Would you hand out credit to every person who walked in your store?

HASKELL: No, but Milton —

MILTON: Don't be childish, Haskell. It can't be done.

HASKELL: Thirty years ago, maybe half a million Jews came here every year —

MILTON: Along with the ghettos and crowded slums —

HASKELL: —and last year they let in five thousand refugees from Eastern Europe.

HASKELL:	MILTON:
Five thousand.	Five thousand, fine.
	Five million, no.

HASKELL: *(To* IMA*)* Does that sound like the doors are open?

IMA: I think we ought not to talk politics if it's the Sabbath.

LEAH: Haskell, she's right.

HASKELL: Doesn't fix anything to say you can't talk about it.

MILTON: All right now, wait a second. Let's not forget that you cost me a lot of money before you cleared your slate.

LEAH: IMA:
Mr. Perry!   Milton!

MILTON: Now, wait a second! And I was happy to do it. But if there had been two of you or more, a man'd have to stop and think about it, now wouldn't he?

HASKELL: In other words, you're only ready to help somebody if it's easy.

MILTON: You're calling me a selfish man, and I resent that, goddamnit. Only a fool would carry generosity to the point of stupidity.

HASKELL: This isn't business, Milton, it's people. We could provide for more than five thousand people a year. Any child could figure that. They don't have to crowd into Hester Street. They don't have get on relief. We didn't.

MILTON: Well, you're an exceptional case, Haskell.

HASKELL: We're not a case, Milton. We're people —

LEAH: HASKELL:
Haskell, you're being   —.and I'm not
silly. It's Shabbos,   exceptional, I'm normal.
for God's sake.

HASKELL: I'm the same as everybody trying to get in. If I were immigrating today, I wouldn't even pass customs. They demand a literacy test now. They demand only skilled laborers. No, the fact is, the United States is a castle. The moat on one side is the Pacific

Ocean, the other side is the Atlantic. And the suffering of people? A rumor in the newspaper.

MILTON: You stood in my yard with your hand held out and I helped you.

HASKELL: Yes, I know that.

MILTON: You take care of business in your own home.

HASKELL: I take care at home!

MILTON: You got trouble with your boy, makes you forget yourself.

HASKELL: Sometimes trouble, yes. But I keep my family together. You have no right to tell me about *my* son!

LEAH: Shah! Haskell!

MILTON: Well, we'd best be going.

IMA: Oh honey, now please. Let's just change the subject.

MILTON: I'll be damned if I'm going to sit here and be preached at and especially from you. Where the hell would you be if it wasn't for me?

HASKELL: I'm not a child, Milton.

MILTON: Nobody has ever given me a goddamn thing.

IMA: MILTON:
That's not true,   So if I want to
Milton!   keep my yard —

MILTON: — clean of every damn stray dog in the world, what the hell business is it of yours?

HASKELL: Go on, then! Go live your life.

MILTON: Come on.

HASKELL: You've helped me. I'm grateful. Why should you do anything more?

MILTON: Ima, let's go!

(*He leaves.*)

IMA: I really think I oughta....

LEAH: No, Ima, please don't. I'm fine. I promise. I'll talk to you. I'm so sorry.

HASKELL: *(After they've gone)* I've paid my debt to you! I don't owe you a goddamn thing!

(In a fury, he blows out the candles.)

Scene Six

(A projection of the town square, a busy day in 1940. Harelik's Dry Goods can be seen, as well as The Perry National Bank. We hear the traffic quietly passing. The lights slowly reveal the HARELIK front porch. HASKELL is replacing some loose slates in the porch railing. LEAH enters from the street with three bolts of red cloth.)

LEAH: Well, the cloth came for the graduation gowns.

HASKELL: Oh, good. Finally.

LEAH: I was afraid we didn't order enough, but Jimmy Wiley's being held back a grade, so there's just enough.

HASKELL: Who's working on them? Are you going to have it by Sunday?

LEAH: We'll have it. It's all arranged.

HASKELL: All right.

LEAH: I thought Ima might like to help out, since Milton's graduating.

HASKELL: You should ask her.

LEAH: I did.

HASKELL: Oh, good.

LEAH: I just saw her down at the square. She didn't know he was graduating. I was embarrassed for her, Haskell.

HASKELL: Well, we should invite them.

LEAH: You know Milton can't go.

HASKELL: Well, invite Ima, then.

LEAH: She scared me. I don't think she gets out anymore.

HASKELL: Leah, if you want to invite Ima to the graduation, then do it. You don't need my permission.

LEAH: What do you want, Haskell?

HASKELL: I'd like to finish this before midnight, so the house won't fall down, if I could.

LEAH: She asked if you would come over.

HASKELL: Well, we should sometime.

LEAH: She asked for tonight.

HASKELL: I don't think so.

LEAH: Why?

HASKELL: I just don't think it's a good idea.

LEAH: Why? *(He works in silence.)* You don't have an answer.

HASKELL: I don't have an answer because it's not worth discussing, Leah.

LEAH: It's not worth it that Ima is frightened and alone in that house with a very sick man?

HASKELL: Leah, please. I'm sorry for that, too. But Milton and I are different people. We're different from each other. We're different from what we were. It's best to recognize that.

LEAH: Are you comfortable with this, Haskell?

HASKELL: Yes.

LEAH: Then you're the only one.

(She goes in.)

Scene Seven

(A projection is seen of young MILTON *in a long red graduation gown.)*

RADIO ANNOUNCER: ...and here's a little reminder from Haskell Harelik's Department Store in Hamilton that it's not too late to remember the graduate in your family. This week they're featuring those good Red Goose Foot Builder shoes.

(The projection changes to an interior of the Harelik store, with stacks of anklets in the foreground.)

RADIO ANNOUNCER: And for the girl grad, they've got those class year anklet socks she's been asking about, with her graduating year monogrammed right on the top.

(The lights reveal the PERRY *porch. The* RADIO ANNOUNCER*'s voice is coming from a radio next to* MILTON*'s chair.* IMA *comes out the door and looks down the street.)*

RADIO ANNOUNCER: So if you want to come in and browse, or maybe just get in out of the heat, I know ol' Haskell is always glad to see you. That's the word from Haskell Harelik's on the south side of the square in Hamilton.

(Texas swing music begins playing and continues until the radio is shut off. We hear a car pull up. IMA *waves.)*

IMA: *(Calling into the house)* They're here, hon! Hey, y'all, hello!

LEAH: *(O.S.)* Hello! *(We hear the slam of a car door.)*

IMA: Haskell, you can park around by the well, that'll be fine.

*(*LEAH *enters.)*

IMA: So, come on up. All right, well, here we are.

(LEAH *hands her a wicker basket.*)

IMA: Oh, now what's this?

LEAH: Bagels.

IMA: Oh, I was hoping it was bagels! That last batch you made? We went through it in about a day, I'll swan if we didn't.

LEAH: *(A mason jar is also in the basket.)* And this is plum jelly from our trees.

IMA: Well now you're making me feel bad. You didn't have to bring anything.

LEAH: Oh, hush.

IMA: Well, come on up.

(HASKELL *enters, but holds back.*)

IMA: I thought we'd set out on the porch, the weather's so nice. He just won't get out. This'll be good for him.

HASKELL: Hello, Ima.

IMA: *(She goes to him and takes his hand.)* Well, back to the old stomping grounds, I guess, huh?

HASKELL: What happened to the well?

IMA: What? Oh, I tell you. There's been so many kids playing around that durn thing, I had Milton put that slab over the top of it. We haven't used it for years, anyway. Well, I thought we'd set out on the porch, the weather's so nice. I'll go in and roust him out.

(*She props open the door with a small potted plant.*)

IMA: We're so excited y'all are here!

(*She goes in.*)

LEAH: Those bagels!

HASKELL: *(Distracted)* They're fine.

LEAH: Are you all right?

HASKELL: Yeah, it's just — it's hard.

LEAH: I know. *(She puts her head on his shoulder.)* Thank you.

IMA: *(O.S.)* All right, now, here we go.

(She pushes MILTON *onto the porch in a wheelchair. He is completely incapacitated, wearing a hunter's cap, heavy jacket, and slippers.* LEAH *firmly takes* HASKELL's *elbow.)*

IMA: Here's Leah and Haskell.

LEAH: Hello, Milton.

HASKELL: Hello, Milton, how are you?

(There is no response from MILTON.*)*

IMA: He's just an old crank, that's what he is.

*(*LEAH *joins them on the porch.* HASKELL *remains at a distance.)*

IMA: Well, you know, I never realized little Milton was already graduating.

LEAH: Oh, isn't that just amazing?

IMA: That is just the most amazing thing. Well, Dora, I guess he's off to college or what?

LEAH: The Texas University, where else?

IMA: You're gonna have a quiet house.

LEAH: Well, but in the meantime, he and his friends have started this band, and it's just awful. The Clodhoppers.

IMA: The Clodhoppers!

LEAH: They play twingy twangy songs about chickens and plowing behind a mule. You could go crazy.

HASKELL: The first Jewish hillbilly.

LEAH: So what does he know about chickens and mules?

HASKELL: He wants to be like the other boys. It's no fun just to live in the town. That's not a real Texan.

IMA: Well, he'd think different if he had to shovel out a stall or two before breakfast every morning.

HASKELL: Well, sure.

IMA: What a lovely day this turned out to be. Let's go out in the yard, you want to?

(She takes LEAH's hand and they move off alone.)

IMA: He don't look good. I just can't get him to help.

LEAH: Ima, can't he talk?

IMA: Oh, he can talk all right. But he goes up and down. I guess.... I'm scared. I brought our pastor over to talk to him. He's not really a member of the church. He hadn't ever been baptized. Such a silly thing. You'd think he grew up in a cave. But now it's become....He just won't do it. If he dies without....

HASKELL: It's been a good week at the store. Very good.

IMA: *(To LEAH)* Let's go see what those bagels'll do, you want to?

(IMA and LEAH go into the house. On the way, IMA shuts off the radio.)

HASKELL: *(To MILTON)* The rain is good. Farmers and ranchers. It rains, they spend. Benefits everybody. Business is good, though. Fifteen percent up. Denim especially, but that's the war. Oh. Mo, Morty. In the service. Yeah, real soldiers. See?

(He displays the photos in his wallet, holding them carefully before MILTON.)

Oh. Look, look, look. The Navy. First Harelik in a boat in,...hoo!

(MILTON seems to see the pictures, then turns slightly away. Pause.)

I don't know whose mistake this is. Nobody's, but....We see the world too different, I guess. Believe different. Come from....

You're right, what you said, Milton. I came to this town like a dog. I licked your hand. I hid in your house. My wife came and found me there and I was ashamed. Ashamed before her and ashamed before you.

Leah. She had to give up more than I could repay. But she's very strong, you know. She made me forget how much I owe her. For you, I couldn't forget. Not just the money — everything. But there comes a time when you have to say, "No more. I've paid you back. Let me be a man!"

You son of a bitch. You saved my life. I wish I could save yours.

IMA: *(O.S.)* Well, they came out real good.

(LEAH and IMA come onto the porch, with some toasted bagels and a dish of preserves. HASKELL moves away.)

IMA: So come on and help yourselves, everybody.

LEAH: Except I busted the wax in the jelly, so look out. There's still some little pieces.

HASKELL: Leah, I think we can go now.

IMA: Oh, no, now y'all don't have to go so soon, do you?

LEAH: Haskell?

HASKELL: We had a good visit, Ima. A real good visit.

LEAH: Is anything...?

HASKELL: No. Let's go.

(LEAH nods to IMA.)

IMA: Well, all right, then. We're so glad y'all came over.

(LEAH and HASKELL start to go.)

IMA: I just love you.

(They stop. HASKELL, after a long moment, approaches MILTON.)

HASKELL: Goodbye, Milton.

LEAH: Goodbye, Milton. You take care of yourself.

HASKELL: *(To* IMA*)* Goodbye.

LEAH: We'll see you soon.

IMA: Y'all come.

(They leave. MILTON *slightly raises one hand.)*

MILTON: Goodbye.

IMA: Haskell!

(But they're gone.)

IMA: He says goodbye.

Scene Eight

(We hear the Calvary Baptist Church congregation singing a slower version of "Where Shall I Be?" *There is a projected photograph of the three Harelik sons —one in a Navy uniform, one in an Army uniform, one in an Army Air Corps uniform. Appearing and fading away on either side of them are clippings from the Hamilton newspaper—photos of local boys killed, shot down, drowned, imprisoned, missing in action. As these images continue, the lights reveal* LEAH *in her kitchen, preparing the Sabbath challah. It is 1942.)*

IMA: *(O.S.)* Leah, honey, are you home?

LEAH: Ima?

IMA: *(O.S.)* Yes.

LEAH: I'm in the kitchen. Come on back.

*(*IMA *enters.)*

LEAH: How's the working woman?

IMA: Oh! How can you cook in this heat?

LEAH: Shabbos.

IMA: Dora. This was Friday, wasn't it? Where has the week gone? The working woman has sore feet.

LEAH: How did you do today?

IMA: I sold a handbag and two longline girdles. Period. I never realized they actually had to get out there and sell.

LEAH: You just take your time. Haskell is so happy to have you in the store.

IMA: I'm sure I'm only in the way down there —

LEAH: No.

IMA: —but I tell you, I was losing my mind — wandering around the house. I'd stop and stand in one place for the longest time. You know, I've never really worked in my life. I don't think anyone but Haskell would let me get in the way like I'm doing.

LEAH: You're not in the way, Ima!

IMA: Well, uh huh.

(Pause)

IMA: Let me do something here, darling. What can I do?

LEAH: Here. This dough is about ready to punch down.

IMA: Oh, good. I'll make like this is that new fellow from Fort Worth that moved into the old Embry place.

(She gives the dough a stout whack.)

IMA: He bought the bank today.

LEAH: Ima, what? You sold the bank?

IMA: I'll tell you something I found out. Learn your husband's business. When I saw all those papers and documents and holdings and trusts....It's not that he left me in a mess. He just never expected to die. Really. You don't know. But the main thing is I want to be away from the bank. You look at those rock walls and it has his face.

(Pause)

IMA: Did we hear from little Milton today?

LEAH: Morty's on a boat in the Pacific, you know. Mo, Mr. Hotrod, still driving a tank in Africa. And my baby? Who knows. The Air Corps. Big secret.

IMA: Couldn't you just spit? I'll swan, if I'd had the salt to slap him sometimes, I'd a-done it. He never did accept Jesus. I begged him. "You don't know what you're doing. You can't die without Jesus." "No," he said, "No. I don't need any help."

He lay there all those weeks and I could see God's hand on him. He got thinner and thinner until his poor soul just lay shimmering on the bed. And he was so scared. "Take the comforting hand of Jesus. I can't go with you, but Jesus can. Just believe." "No," he said. "For me, then, do it for me. How can you die without Jesus?" And all he would say was, "No. No. No."

He's lost, Leah. His blessed soul is lost. How can God let that happen? What is heaven if my husband isn't there? My God, then I don't want it. I don't want it.

(LEAH *has her arms around* IMA.)

IMA: What do I do?

(*As the women hold each other,* HASKELL *enters the front yard. He carries a shovel and a tall, scrawny sapling, its roots bound in burlap. He calls inside.*)

HASKELL: Leah?

LEAH: Yes, Haskell?

HASKELL: Leah, come out here.

LEAH: What is it?

HASKELL: Just come out here. I need you for a minute.

IMA: Just a minute, Haskell. Ima's here.

HASKELL: Oh, good. I need both of you.

LEAH: Well....

IMA: No, no. I'll be right there, just let me set a second.

LEAH: *(Leaving the kitchen)* What's the big rush?

HASKELL: Well, come out here and you'll see.

(IMA composes herself in the kitchen. LEAH comes onto the porch.)

LEAH: So what's so important out here?

HASKELL: *(He's putting the sapling into a hole in the ground.)* I got the tree.

LEAH: This little stick?

HASKELL: Don't wither it before it's in the ground. Come hold it up so I can get the dirt in.

(IMA comes onto the porch.)

HASKELL: Oh, good, Ima. I'm glad you're here.

LEAH: It's for the boys. But why all of a sudden? Did you hear something? Is something wrong?

HASKELL: Now don't start getting excited.

LEAH: Tell me!

HASKELL: *(He takes a telegram from his shirt pocket.)* This telegram came to the store right after you left. Go on. Read it.

LEAH: "Arrived London safe and sound. Will write soon. Love, Milton" Oh, thank you. Thank you.

HASKELL: So I thought it would be a good time.

LEAH: It's so puny. I hope it'll take.

HASKELL: All right, let's see how it looks.

(The tree stands alone.)

IMA: Well, just look at it, would you?

HASKELL: Yeah, not bad.

It's funny, you know. We usually plant a tree as a kind of memory. We look at it and we think back. The jujubee for Morty, the plum tree for Mo, plum tree for

Milton—newborn babies. I can hear them crying, me acting like a complete case, Mr. Perry with his cigar.

(He turns to the tree.)

But you, I want to look at you and think ahead. I want you to stand up straight, fifty years, a hundred years—stretch your branches to Heaven so Heaven can hear. We gave back.

(HASKELL and LEAH hold each other.)

Mama, we gave back.

(He recites a blessing in Hebrew, then with his fingertips, plants a kiss on an upper leaf. He looks at his watch.)

All right, it's almost time! I'm starving to death. Ima, I'm glad you're here. Will you stay for Shabbos?

IMA: If that's all right.

HASKELL: Of course, it's all right.

(LEAH is still intent upon the tree. He speaks quietly to IMA.)

I'll go wash up. Smuts, shmuts, shmutsik.

(He goes in.)

LEAH: This is for Mordechai.

(She plants a kiss on a small leaf.)

LEAH: This is for Moishe.

(Another kiss)

LEAH: And this is for Milton.

(Another kiss)

IMA: For Milton.

(She plants a kiss. The clear cry of a mockingbird fills the air. As the women stand in the silence, a projection of MILTON HARELIK, in a military portrait, appears. The actor who played HASKELL now enters as his son, MILTON, dressed as in the photograph, carrying an officer's flight bag. He comes into the HARELIK yard.)

MILTON HARELIK: Mama's prayer did not go unanswered. I came back from that war, and so did my older brothers, safe and sound. And after they married and moved away, I stayed right here in Hamilton and watched that puny little stick they planted in 1942 grow strong and tall. In fact, that tree and I have sort of become permanent fixtures in this town.

(He sees a projection of himself and HASKELL, *from a newspaper clipping.)*

1955. I took over the dry goods store as Papa slowed down. I say slowed down. He just shifted his activities back home. The grandkids started coming.

(We see projections of HASKELL *and* LEAH *with their children's children — playing, graduating, honoring Bar Mitzvah....)*

And those kids had children of their own. I guess he's got eleven great-grandchildren now. A lot of little footprints around the place. Footprints. And Mama's old snapshots.

(A projection lingers—a fuzzy snapshot of an elderly LEAH *and* HASKELL. *He looks at it for a moment.)*

1971. I took that one. It's the last picture in our album of the two of them together. Mama passed away about five months after that, and my wife and I moved into the master bedroom—the one I was born in.

(The picture fades away.)

You know, it's funny. It seems that in the years since I took that picture, Papa has become an immigrant once again.

(We hear the ghostly, distant balalaika.)

His mind has finally let go of the house, the store, the family, and floats freely now back to Russia.

(A projection of the little yeshiva boy from the prologue appears.)

Back to his boyhood home. To the cedar forests and the
thatched-roof village — the green and simple times of
his childhood. He speaks only Yiddish now. And he
claims to hear balalaikas in the morning. He rarely
recognizes me and the kids anymore, and Hamilton
seems, well, foreign to him.

(A projection of HASKELL's *elderly face is superimposed for a
moment over the little boy's face. They become one, then the
boy fades away.* MILTON *looks at it.)*

September, 1985. The occasion of his ninety-eighth
birthday. We had a little party for him and that evening
we took him for a drive around town and we ended up
down at the square. We took a turn in front of the
store —

(A projection of the storefront and the sign, Haskell
Harelik's, *appears.)*

— and I was trying to get him to recognize it. I pointed
to the name he put up seventy-five years ago. "You see
that big ol' sign up there, Papa? That's you! That's your
name up there! Dein nohmen!" He looked at it. "Mein
nohmen," he said. "Mein nohmen?"

We sat there in the car for several minutes. Nobody said
a word. He didn't remember his name. He didn't
remember any of it. And not quite two years later, he
was gone.

*(He watches the projection slowly fade away. He picks up his
flight bag and heads for the house. The mockingbird calls to
him and he stops on the porch to look for it. He and the tree
are in two pools of light for a moment, then the stage fades to
black.)*

END OF PLAY

SONGS & PRAYERS

DI GRINE KUSINE

Tsu mir iz gekummen ah kusine
Shain vie golt iz zie gevain di greene
Baykelach vie roite pomerantzen
Fiselach vos betten zich tsum tantsen

Zie iz nit gegangen nor geshprungen
Zie hot nit gerett nor gezungen
Fraylich lustik iz gevain ihr meene
Ot azoy gevain iz mein kusine

Herelach in goldene gelockte
Tsaindelach vie perelach getockte
Oigelach vie teibelach ah tsvilling
Lipelach vie karshelach in frilling

Ich hob zich bakent mit mein nextdorke
Zie hot gehot a millinery storke
A job hob gekrigen far di greene
Az leben zol Columbus's medine

Paide hot zie a lange tseit geklieben
Fin mein kusine iz ah helft gebliben
Die baykelach vie roite pomerantzen
Hoben zich shoin ois gegreent in gantsen

A boy hot zie zich shoin ois gefinnen
Er hot bei ihr die paide tsegenimmen
Oif yeden shrit un trit flaig er zie vatchen
Yede nacht flaig er zie gut ois patchen

Es iz shoin fargangen ah pur yohren
Fin mein kusine iz a tell gevoren
Unter ihre bloye shaine oigen
Shvartse passen hoben zich getsoigen

Yetst az ich begaigen mein kusine
Fraig ich ihr vos machst du epes greene
Entfert zie mir mit ah troirige meene
Az brenen zol Columbus's medine

by Hyman Prizant and Abe Schwartz
© Copyright 1922 by Joneil Music Co.

DI GRINE KUSINE
(The Greenhorn Cousin)

Once a cousin came to me
Pretty as gold was she, the greenhorn,
Cheeks like red candy
Tiny feet begging to dance

She didn't walk, but skipped
She didn't talk, but sang
Her manner was gay and cheerful
That's how my cousin used to be

Hair in golden locks
Little teeth like a string of pearls
Little eyes like twin doves
Little lips like spring cherries

I introduced her to my neighbor
The one with a millinery store
I got a job for my cousin
Long life to Columbus's land

She worked many years for wages
Until only half of her was left
The cheeks like red candy
Now were only green

She found herself a boy
He took away all her money

He watched every move she made
Every night he beat her

The years have now gone by
My cousin has become a wreck
Under her pretty blue eyes
Black lines are now drawn

Now when I meet my cousin
I ask, how are you, greenhorn
She says with a sorrowful face
To hell with Columbus's land

Translation by Mark Harelik

WHERE SHALL I BE?

Chorus: When judgment day is drawing nigh,
Where shall I be?
And God the works of men shall try, oh,
Where shall I be?
When east to west the fire shall roll,
Where shall I be?
How will it be with my poor souls, oh,
Where shall I be?

Refrain: Where shall I be when that first trumpet
sounds?
Tell me where shall I be when it sounds so loud?
When it sounds so loud as to wake up the dead,
Tell me where shall I be when it sounds?

When wicked men His wrath shall see,
Where shall I be?
And to the hills and mountains flee, oh,
Where shall I be?
When rocks and mountain fall away,
Where shall I be?
And all the works of men decay, oh,
Where shall I be?

(Refrain)

All trouble gone, all conflict passed,
Where shall I be?
And old Appolyon bound at last, oh,
Where shall I be?
When love shall reach from shore to shore,
Where shall I be?
And peace abide forever more, oh,
Where shall I be?

(Refrain)

Sabbath Blessing for the Candles

Boruch Atoh, Adoshem, Elokaynu melech ho'olom,
ashehr kidshonuh b'mitsohsohv l'hadlik nehr shel
Shabbos. (Blessed are You, Hashem, our God, King of
the Universe, Who sanctified us with His
commandments, and has commanded us to kindle the
light of the Sabbath.)

Sabbath Blessing for the Children

Y'simcho Elokim k'Ephrayim v'chi Menasheh.
Y'vorehcho Adoshem v'yishmorecho. Yo-ehr Adoshem
ponov elechu vichunecho. Yiso Adoshem ponov elecho,
v'yosaym l'cho shalom. (May God make you like
Ephraim and Menashe. May Hashem bless you and
safeguard you. May Hashem illuminate His
countenance for you and be gracious to you. May
Hashem turn his countenance to you and establish
peace for you.)

Kiddush

Boruch Atoh, Adoshem, Elokaynu melech ho'olom,
boray pree hagohfen. (Blessed are You, Hashem, our
God, King of the Universe, Who creates the fruit of the
vine.)

Boruch Atoh, Adoshem, Elokaynu melech ho'olom,
ashehr kih d'shonu b'mitsosohv v'rotsovonu,
[v'shabbos kohd'sho b'ah-havo oovrotson hihnchilonu,
zikoron l'ma-asay v'rayshees. Kih hoo yom t'chiloh

l'mikro-ay kodesh, zaychehr litsi-ahs mitsroyihm. kih
vonu v'chartoh, v'ohsohnu kidashtoh, mikohl
ha'amihm.] V'shabbos kohdsh'cho b'ah-havo oovrotson
hihnchaltohnu. Boruch atoh Adoshem, mikadesh
hashabbos. (Blessed are You, Hashem, our God, King of
the Universe, Who has sanctified us with His
commandments, took pleasure in us, and with love and
favor gave us His holy Sabbath as a heritage, a
remembrance of creation. For that day is the prologue
to the holy convocations, a memorial of the Exodus
from Egypt. For us did You choose and us did You
sanctify from all nations. And Your holy Sabbath, with
love and favor, did You give us as a heritage. Blessed
are You, Hashem, Who sanctifies the Sabbath.)

*Note: In the original production, the bracketed passage was
deleted for time purposes only.*

Blessing for the Bread

Boruch Atoh, Adoshem, Elokaynu melech ho'olom,
hamotseh lechem mihn ho'oretz. (Blessed are You,
Hashem, our God, King of the Universe, Who brings
forth bread from the earth.)

Blessing for the Tree

Boruch Atoh, Adoshem, Elokaynu melech ho'olom,
shehecheyonu v'kimohnu, v'higiyohnu lazmahn hazeh.
(Blessed are you, Hashem, our God, King of the
Universe, Who has kept us alive, sustained us, and
brought us to this season.)

*Note: The pronunciations of Adoshem and Elokaynu have
been altered according to the traditional Jewish premise that a
prayer must never be uttered in vain. Therefore, when used
in a theatrical context, the blessing is changed in this slight
way to become a representation of the prayer and not the
prayer itself.*